Jukeboxes & Jackalopes

A Wyoming Bar Journey

Julianne Couch

The essay "A Horse of a Different Color"
appears in a slightly different form in the
2007 Owen Wister Review.

Cover Design & Image: Horse Creek Studio
Photography: Ronald Hansen
Published by Pronghorn Press

www.pronghornpress.org

October 8, 2007

To Cheryl —

Mom says you get
homesick —

I hope this helps

This book's for you.

Cheers!
Juli-anne Cover

Table of Contents

Acknowledgements

This book was a work in progress in my mind well before the writing began. Several people listened to me describe the project and encouraged me with words like, "Great idea—I wish I'd thought of that!" Thank you to Jane Nelson, Jim Wangberg, and Lindy Griffith and to my mentor Keith Denniston, who never knew about this project but inspired me nevertheless.

Others provided support and encouragement as I toured from bar to bar and struggled to make my writing do justice to each. These folks include Bob and Carolyn Young, Brian and Dana Eberhard, Suzanne Bopp, and John Freeman.

Still others stepped up to help me along with the details of making this assortment of essays into a book. Jeffe Kennedy, RoseMarie London, Kevin Holdsworth, Vicki Lindner and Alyson Hagy: thanks for helping me figure out how to do this.

Countless friends and family members listened to Ron and me babble on about the wonderful folks we'd met in Wyoming bars. Friends and family: thanks for listening. Bar folks: thanks for talking.

Travel from bar to bar around the great state of Wyoming is not an inexpensive prospect: thanks to the University of Wyoming Department of English, the College of Arts and Sciences, and the Wyoming Arts Council, for their support.

Thanks to my friend Stephen Donatelli, who I met by chance and who, through his meticulous comments on an early draft, helped me see what kind book it was I wanted to write.

It isn't an overstatement to say this bar book would not have been written without my husband, photographer and fellow bar tourist Ronald K. Hansen. We walked into each bar together, and left together, too!

Last but never least, our little white dog Spike was along for the ride to each and every bar—he makes all journeys fun.

Introduction

If one isn't allergic to cigarette smoke and doesn't mind the muffled boom of a jukebox that sounds like it spent time at the bottom of the sea, there's no better way to learn about a place and the people who pass through it than spending some time in the local bar.

Bars, saloons, taverns: they go by many names signed over doors and etched on windows, or printed on napkins if the place is swanky. Regardless of name they are, in fact, an inner sanctum of their community. Unlike churches, where people go to think about something other than themselves, or jobs, where people go to think about making money for someone else, bars are where people go to think about enjoying themselves for awhile. That's not such a bad thing.

Time spent in a bar can mean time away from the weather, or job demands, or just from the ordinary. It can mean making a friendship that lasts an hour. It can mean getting together with old friends to catch up on the week. And yes, it can and usually does mean drinking, although it doesn't have to mean drunkenness. In fact, it is drunkenness that gives bars a bad name.

I am not a barfly. My college days of weekend dissipation are in the dim past, and thinking about my episodes of girls-night-out for dancing with strangers gives me a vague queasy headache. These days I confine my bar-going to infrequent occasions and try to get home before the second hand cigarette smoke welds together the tissue of my nostrils. At least, that was true until I got the idea for a bar tour.

One of the pleasures of life, for me, is to drop by a bar when visiting a new place. The best time is during the day, when only a few cars or motorcycles are in the parking lot. Entering a bar as a stranger under the full glare of the sun is not for people who can't endure a stare. I don't mind, though, for I can gawk along with the best of them, and drink a beer during the day, and enter a conversation with strangers. But that last is the hardest part, because I'd much rather follow my inclination to dawdle in a corner, listening and watching.

Sometimes nothing much happens so there isn't much to see. Bartenders serve drinks, usually beer. If the phone rings, they answer it. They almost always smoke from a position near the end of the bar. People come in and sit at the bar, occupying every other stool if they don't know one another, or if they are men who don't want to appear overly fond of their male companions. Sometimes the people don't talk much but instead stare at the TV set, whether or not the sound is on.

The isolation and quiet and monotony can go on like that without break. But then the snow can start to fall and bar patrons can marvel at the flakes slashing horizontally up the street from the direction of the railroad tracks. A taxicab can pull up to the bar, one of the few vehicles still trekking through the storm. And out of that taxicab can step a man and woman in full biker regalia: black leather jackets and black leather chaps. And in they can come into the bar, dressed to ride but settling for being driven, then have a drink. Am I the only one who notes the irony of donning anti-road burn gear, then hailing the closest taxi? I don't know if I am or not, because no one comments, at least not aloud. In bars like this acceptance of others is the first rule.

Most people want to live in a community that feels comfortable and welcoming to them, and some people have the good fortune to find such a place. I am one of those people, and I came to Wyoming to settle in 1992.

I didn't come for a job or school or to be near someone near and dear. No, I left a job and family in Kansas City to live here, where I had nearly nothing. Why? I felt at home here, in part because of time I'd spent in a certain bar during the numerous Wyoming vacations that led up to my move.

From the first I could detect a compatible ambiance between my favorite Kansas City bar and this particular watering hole in Laramie. There wasn't much physical similarity—the bar in Kansas City was large and sprawling with lots of rooms added on where walls had been knocked down. The one in Laramie was small with one main room and a back area for storage. The bar in Kansas City once catered to Irish clientele, but at some point grew widely popular as the neighborhood where it was situated became gentrified. The bar in Laramie catered to, well, bikers and people who liked to fight. At least that was its reputation, but as a visiting stranger I wasn't tainted by that info. The bar in Kansas City was once a favorite hangout of the painter Thomas Hart Benton, and several of his works adorned the walls between beer lights and posters for local sports teams. The walls of the place in Laramie sported stuffed big game heads and full body poses of smaller dear-departed animals, some with more heads or legs than natural. This bar's hero was a man who local legend says passed away there while drinking, and his last bottle rests on a shelf near the barstools like a painted icon in a niche.

The contrasts between the two places seem significant, but they really are not, when you consider the similarities. It was those similarities that made me visit the Laramie bar every time I passed through here. And it is those similarities that make me visit the Kansas City bar every time I'm there to see family and friends. In both places I feel no need for pretense. If I want to lurk in dark corners gaping at strangers, I can do that. If I want to perch on a high stool and chat with the bartender, I can do that. If I want to go in and order a beer at ten a.m.... well, I ordinarily wouldn't want to do that, but I certainly could if I wished. And the freedom isn't mine alone. If a bachelorette party wants to invade the bar in full wedding garb in the company of a life-sized blow-up groom, and take over the suggestion of a dance floor in front of the jukebox, singing and swinging for ten minutes before heading back out, they can do that. In fact on a trip to Kansas City to visit family and make a pilgrimage to the bar, that exact thing happened. It was met with the same day-in-the-life acceptance with which the taxied bikers were greeted a few years before at the Laramie bar. It is the culture of acceptance in both places that make anything possible, and makes going there darn interesting.

Better than any Chamber of Commerce office or tourist information hut, these bars are where people in the know stop by to find out what the place is really all about. And isn't that really the goal of visiting new places? We already know what McDonald's is like, no offense to predictability. But don't we want to know what the people there are really like, walking around in their metaphorical underwear behind closed doors? A visit to the local watering hole is a great way to learn.

What follows in this book is a sampling of some of the more out of the way community gathering spots in my adopted state of Wyoming. They are presented in no particular order. The book intentionally leaves out some of the more well known places that the traveler may venture into on the advice of a tourism promotion or the recommendation of a billboard. It also leaves out bars in larger towns, where gathering places are plenty, and people spend more than enough time meeting one another in the usual locations and thus don't need to go to bars for company. The focus of this book is on the small, the easily overlooked, the kind of place where passersby might remark to one another "How does that place stay in business?" All of these locations have their own stories, their own patrons, and their own place in the community of Wyoming. Each location taught me something about myself and affirmed the reasons I cling to life in Wyoming, like a wildflower clings to a granite outcropping. I hope those lessons resonate for readers, as you search for your own perfect place to grow.

In the best sense, all of Wyoming has become for me, over the years, like one big bar, a community center where I am welcome to find a corner to sit and watch with fine fun surprise as the extraordinary and ordinary rub elbows and make acquaintance with one another, if only for the day. This book is my toast to them. Cheers!

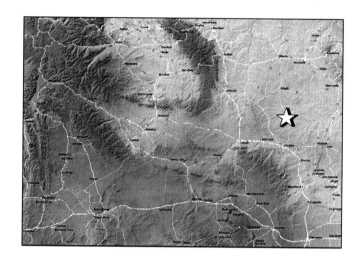

Bar in View! O the Joy!
Dry Creek Saloon
Bill, Wyoming

Have you been to the bar in Bill? Oh, you have to go to the Bill Yacht Club. You haven't been to a Wyoming bar until you've been to Bill.

Sometimes the most memorable part of a trip is the journey itself. It's being in the back seat of the car, at the mercy of parents, wondering if they'll ever stop for lunch, to find a bathroom, or just to stretch restless legs. It's playing the license plate game to relieve the sameness of an endless interstate highway. It's opening powdered Sweet Tarts packaged in stiff paper straws, pouring them down the throat and trying not to choke as molecules of sour sugar-dust swell the taste buds and fill the esophagus. It's fighting for turf in the crowded back seat of a 1965 Chevy Malibu, drawing an imaginary line from the hump on the floor across the vinyl bench seat, on up to the back dash, which no sisters or sisters' personal effects may cross. Dialog from such trips always includes the lines "Are we there yet?" and "Don't make me come back there," spoken from either side of the border of a front seat that rises like the Wailing Wall above the heads of young back seat passengers.

These are the images I recall from childhood travels. I can still feel the back of my legs sticking to the vinyl seat of the Malibu. I can see Sweet Tart dust particles suspended in the Midwestern sunshine that poured through the windows of the un-air-conditioned car. I can remember trying to concentrate on *Archie* comics and *Mad Magazine* while my sister whined about car sickness. Whenever we complained of being hungry, my mother the peacemaker tried to quiet our groans so that they didn't distract my father, who was Driving. She fed us Space Food sticks: rubbery sugary protien-y concoctions developed for orbiting astronauts. If they were good enough for the crew of the Apollo, they should surely keep us going until we arrived at the motel.

And where was this motel? Where did we go for family vacations each year of my childhood? Beats me. I recall very little, beyond Holiday Inn swimming pools, doting relatives, and one really bad earache that kept me glued with pain to the floor of my aunt's living room. But boy, do I remember the inside of that car, and all the miles we logged.

A recent trip to Bill similarly affects me as an odyssey in which the journey, and the characters met along the way, are a bigger part of the story than our experience of the bar itself. For one thing, my husband Ron and I had heard so much about the bar in Bill since we'd started telling people about our travels.

Bill is a town with one resident, but plenty of locals living on nearby ranches and in the man-camp set up for railroad workers. It has had a post office since 1919, and in the 1930s the post office expanded into a store that sold packaged beer, which people could buy and then guzzle between the bread aisle and the checkout stand. The Bill Store eventually became known as the Bill Yacht Club, mysteriously dubbed by regulars who would bring along their own hard liquor to mix in with soft drinks they could purchase there.

The place was notorious for quirkiness, even measured by Wyoming's relaxed standards of conformity. A previous owner took to carrying a sidearm in a holster and was ready to use it to manage unruly customers. The name of the town itself seems quirky too, until you know that it was named for four landowners whose property cornered at about this spot. They and the first postmaster were all named Bill.

These days, things around Bill are more "normal." There's a new owner named Mark who doesn't appear to carry a gun, and in fact, holds a regular job driving a big truck at a local coal mine. Mark has cleaned up an area in the rear of the building and, after hauling away several dumpsters-full of decades-old garbage, has a very clean and attractive bar. Black carpet midway up the walls shows the neon beer signs to best effect. A neutral colored concrete floor is easy to keep clean and reflects the light. No stuffed game or mounted trophy heads collect dust and threaten to drop fleas into freshly tapped glasses of beer. Instead, Budweiser goodies fill the bar, and iconography of NASCAR hero Dale Earnhardt Jr., driver of the red number 8 Budweiser Chevy, decorates banners and coasters. Mothers and fathers can now bring their children into the store to load up on provisions without having to pick their way through packs of inebriated hunters or tiptoe through gangs of railroad workers. Now those people are socializing safely in the back of the building, in the pleasant bar where up to sixty-two of them at a time can cozy up on barstools or around small tables.

The bar still sells only beer and wine, but customers are no longer encouraged to bring along their own hard-liquor fortification. That would be against Wyoming law. To reflect the normalizing of the place, Mark has even changed the name of the bar to match some other local landmarks and institutions, and he's replaced the yacht and antelope logo. Welcome to the Dry Creek Saloon.

But now we are at the destination port of our journey, Bill. First, we have to plot the course, launch the vessel, and let the Wyoming winds blow us where they may. Before that metaphor strikes anyone as being needlessly romantic and misplaced for the ranching and mining lands of northeastern Wyoming, picture this: We were on an odyssey with a long wide blue fiberglass canoe strapped, keel up, to the top of our Toyota RAV4. We'd taken the canoe along on this trip so that we could do some recreating at Glendo Reservoir, a large lake just north of where we were staying in Guernsey. We canoed at Glendo the morning of our trip to Bill, and then proceeded on northwest along the back roads and through the ranchlands of the Powder River Basin toward the Yacht Club. Like Lewis and Clark's Corps of Discovery, we set out to see what was navigable across a vast jumble of water and earth. We couldn't have appeared any more out of place with our upside down canoe than did the captains and men with their sextant and fiddle. And like the Corps of Discovery, we couldn't have found our way without the help of bemused locals to give us directions, to exchange goods, and shelter us from the elements of a hot Wyoming afternoon.

We could have left Glendo and hopped on Wyoming 59, an ordinary paved two-lane highway that would have been a straight shot to Bill, about fifty miles to the north. But doing so would have put us briefly on Interstate 25. With the canoe strapped to our roof we weren't feeling very comfortable about the stresses of wind and truck turbulence on the interstate. Besides, the practical route would make us miss all the other dots on the map where bars might be tucked. Towns such as Manville, Keeline, Shawnee, Lost Springs, and Lance Creek, each home to just a handful of people, sang to us over the roar of the efficient but risky interstate.

It was at Lost Springs we first pulled into port, to visit the Lost Bar. Alas, we learned the Lost Bar is closed most of the year, except during hunting season, when folks other than crazies on bar tours might stumble in. No matter: we still found information and goods at the Lost Springs Post Office & Antique Store, which occupies the time of the town's one resident.

We stopped into the dim dusty place and showed the proprietor our state map and our Wyoming topographic atlas, which presented contrary theories about what roads went where and what they were called. He gave us country-style directions about the best route to Bill, complete with local place names, instructions to go north instead of left, and lots of red herrings (you'll see a big barn: don't turn there!).

Feeling confident we could follow the directions he gave, we politely browsed through the antiques, most of which were the sorts of things we already had at home and wondered how to dispose of. Then I felt the tug of an object I was meant to have, and let the strong current of fate pull me to a low glass case of salt-and-pepper shaker sets. There among the dog and cats, the penguins, and the twin Eiffel towers sat a shaker set that appeared to have been dropped off the kitchen table once too often. It wasn't the condition that mattered, though. For the shakers present-ed the journey of Lewis and Clark's Corps of Discovery, specifically, a 100th anniversary commemoration of the event, as marked by the Portland Recon of 1905. The pepper shaker depicted a long low building featuring arched doorways and flagged turrets, labeled Liberal Arts Building. The salt shaker portrayed the two captains being guided toward a sun-soaked Pacific Ocean by none other than the flag-draped spirit of Columbia.

When I saw those shakers I knew they were worth every bit of the eight dollars being asked for them. I've long held an interest in the Corps of Discovery, in part because I am a direct descendant of William Clark and a collateral descendant of Meriwether Lewis. As such, I've always fancied that a bit of the explorers' wanderlust runs through my soul, and this bar tour is a tame but still goal-oriented way of taking my ancestors' spirits out for a spin. So I happily purchased the hundred year old talisman from the proprietor, who in an act of good will, threw in a free button, yellow with a faded red cardinal, printed with the words "Get Lost in Lost Springs." Like Lewis and Clark departing the friendly Mandan Village, we left Lost Springs in high spirits, with fresh supplies and a pretty good idea of where we were going.

We headed out of town north on the literally named gravel Twentymile Road. About ten miles along we met the first passing vehicle, a pickup truck headed toward us. We were expecting the back road custom of a finger lifted off the steering wheel for a wave. Instead, the man driving the pickup slowed down to stop and appeared to be suppressing a laugh as he cranked down his driver's side window. We slowed to a stop and put our window down, too.

He took us in, with our out of county plates, our light-duty SUV, and our oversized bottom-up canoe, and said as seriously as he could manage "You folks looking for Glendo?"

He must have thought us a little off course, since the lake was about thirty miles to our south, as the crow flies, and we were headed north.

"Oh no," we crazy tourists assured him, "We've already been to Glendo. Now we're headed to the Yacht Club at Bill!"

Like Lewis and Clark gazing across a vast sea of grassland, we were certain—in spite of local skepticism—that we'd find a navigable route. We might have been premature in convincing the other driver that we weren't lost, for it wasn't long before Twentymile Road shot off in an unadvertised direction and the looked for turn was either too subtle or non-existent. Soon we found ourselves bobbing on the surface of a lightly traveled gravel road through beautiful but seemingly unpeopled ranch land. I rarely use the phrase "middle of nowhere" because I figure if I can get there, it can't be that inaccessible. But I muttered the phrase here, because it was the literal truth about our position somewhere near the Middle Fork of the East Fork of the West Fork of Piney Creek. If I'd been William Clark keeping a journal of the voyage, I might have written "Nothing but grass. Misqueeters teeribul. Could go for a cold beer. Proceeded on."

Tired at last of trying to reckon the state map to the topographic atlas, we pitched both aside and tried following our sense of direction for awhile. Keep going northwest and eventually we'd have to find Wyoming 59, we told ourselves. After all, it was fast becoming one of the busiest highways in the state. What looks on paper like it should be a lightly traveled route south from Gillette through the Powder River Basin over the Thunder Basin National Grasslands and down to the town of Douglas is in fact a rattling rolling route for miners and their apparatus.

The landscape between Bill and Gillette to the north is mostly coal mines, big pits dug in the earth and all the dust and traffic and heavy machinery necessary to move the coal out. And of course trains: because of mining Bill has become a hub for the Burlington Northern Sante Fe and Union Pacific railroads, which haul coal from the Powder River Basin to electric generating stations in the Midwest and beyond. That accounts for the railroad camp, with its own water tower, just past the store. Needless to say, there is no motel in Bill.

But since most of that activity was to the north of Bill, the road's location still eluded us as we bounced along the grasslands of the Basin. At last: another local to help us out, a tour guide as welcome as Sacagawea. A young woman dressed in jeans and working ranch apparel had just climbed aboard a pickup truck nearly the size of the horse trailer she pulled. As she eased out of the gated ranch road onto the slightly more improved road we were following, we hailed her to stop. Windows were lowered and we stated our intention of getting to Bill, if only she'd tell us where it was.

"Do you want the scenic tour way to get there?" she stammered out. For some reason, she wasn't making eye contact with us. She was gazing at a point just over our heads. We wondered if she were slightly deranged.

"If we turn on this road, will we get to Highway 59?"

"If you want, but most people miss the turnoff and wind up at Lance Crick." She still seemed to be looking past us, and now the little blonde girl riding with her in the truck kneeled up in her seat and gaped past us with Christmas morning eyes. Poor thing. Maybe it runs in the family.

"So we should just go that way?" We pointed off into the middle distance.

"If you want to get to Bill."

We thanked her and drove off according to her instructions. We were almost to the highway before we realized the nice lady wasn't unbalanced. She was just trying to figure what we were doing out there, miles from the nearest body of water larger than a stock pond, with a big blue canoe strapped to our roof, looking for the Yacht Club. She was probably still explaining canoes, and tourists, to the little girl when we finally found the highway. I thought of Captain Lewis with his air gun, which he demonstrated to astounded natives on his journey to the Pacific. Surely no expression of astonishment at that invention could have been much greater than what we saw on the face of that toddler.

Ocean in View. O the joy! Echoing William Clark, we gratefully found our destination, the highway, and cued up with the other cars and trucks headed north. After an uneventful twenty miles we arrived at Bill. There were no other customers in the store or the Dry Creek Saloon that afternoon, so were we able to talk with Mark quite a bit as we munched the chili dog and burger he'd fixed and served to us in little paper trays.

He confessed that he bought the bar without realizing quite how much he'd be tied down to it. His full time job at the mine means a fifty mile one-way commute to his home in Douglas each working day. His college-age daughters help run the business and do accounting work, and he has one employee, the woman referred to in the sign that says Population One. She moved into Bill's one house from California to be closer to her daughter's home on a nearby ranch. Mark isn't sure what he'd do if she decided to leave, but he sees an end to the overwork he's enduring now. In just nine more years he'll be eligible to retire from the mine with full benefits. He thinks the railroad might like to buy his property to expand their hub operations, but he prefers to protect the history of this legendary place. He can look out the front window of the store and see the spot where the previous owner died in a highway rollover, just days after selling the place to Mark. He remembers the memorial service held in the Dry Creek Saloon, when sixty-two of the previous owner's customers, now his customers, filled up the place to remember their friend.

Change comes to Wyoming in sputters and starts, not in a gentle progression too subtle for notice. Change has come to Bill, too, in the form of a new owner and a new way of doing things. The Bill Yacht Club that people told us we had to see to believe is a thing of the past. But the Dry Creek Saloon is clean, inviting, friendly, and has a good sense of history about it. You can buy beer there but guzzling it down in the bread aisle is frowned upon.

We eventually said so long to Mark, bought a T-shirt that featured the old Yacht Club logo, and took the quicker but less adventurous way back down the interstate. No one on that highway seemed to notice the canoe.

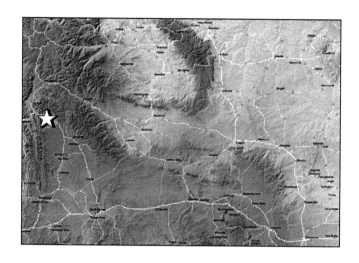

Of Black Bears and Big Macs
Elk Horn Bar
Bondurant, Wyoming

    "...and then the guy said, 'Grand Manures all around!'" Har har har the bar's occupants bust into a laugh. We'd entered the Elk Horn in Bondurant just in time to hear the punch line of a joke from a bar regular named Glenn. Get it? Grand Manure for Grand Marnier, that spicy-sweet orange after-dinner liquor sipped in the fancier establishments of places like Jackson Hole, down Hoback Canyon on the other side of the Gros Ventre Range, another planet from here. Not more than thirty-five miles distant and 600 feet apart in elevation, but Jackson Hole and Bondurant are the antipodes of Wyoming culture.

    Bondurant in summer is sun-soaked ranches and horseback riding and barbecues. In winter it is deep-freeze cold, snowbirds in exodus, and kids sixth grade and up who ride busses more than forty miles each way to school in Pinedale. Bondurant, population 100, elevation 6,209, has a post office, a church, and an elementary school, scattered haphazardly along the Hoback Valley between river and roadway like sticks dropped from the beak of a nest-building eagle.

The Elk Horn is near the north end of the stretch. In addition to being a saloon, the Elk Horn is a restaurant, a convenience store with gas pumps, and cabins for rent. The Elk Horn is where everybody in the area stops, at least once in awhile. It is a destination for summer and winter recreationalists taking advantage of the beautiful unspoiled Bridger-Teton Wilderness Area and nearby national forests. It is a temporary respite for travelers bound for Jackson Hole.

On this November day, I am almost embarrassed to confess, we were in the latter group, bound for a holiday in the Hole. I was on Thanksgiving break from my teaching job, and Ron and I saw a chance to combine some bar visits with a relatively exotic destination. Jackson Hole, wherein lies the town of Jackson, is about seven hours from our town of Laramie in good weather. Not exactly close, but a much easier reach than the homes of our Midwestern relations. We decided to go north and be tourists for awhile.

If Bondurant is all things Western and ranchy and rustic, Jackson Hole is... something else. Pricey world-class downhill ski areas, celebrity residents, wealthy people driving property values up and driving the working class who keep it all going over the border into Idaho. Vacation spot for presidents and international executives. Shopping, ski-resort architecture, art galleries galore, traffic (bearable in winter, god-awful in summer) so uncharacteristic of anyplace else in Wyoming that many in the state dismiss it as "California East." But it was discovered, just like Bondurant was, by mountain men of the hunting and trapping variety, exploring this new (to them) country in the 1800s.

Then called Jackson's Hole, the valley was named by William Sublette after his partner David E. Jackson. Sublette gave his own name to Sublette County, where Bondurant is. Native peoples had inhabited the area for twelve thousand years, and whites found that abundant food sources and shelter suited them just fine, too, at least during the warm months. The white men made their living trapping beaver, but after beaver numbers began to drop and Eastern fashions inclined toward silk, the trappers mostly left the Hole to others. Eventually, though, western exploration was full-press on again, and Mormons and other settlers began filling in the gaps among the tall Teton peaks. The designation of Yellowstone as the nation's first national park prompted tourism, and that activity has been a go ever since.

Mountain man lore opens the first chapter of many western Wyoming town histories, and for many of those towns that's just about all she wrote, up to the present. "Oh yeah, some white guys trapping beaver stumbled upon Valley X, and then the Pony Express came through, and then some ranches came in so they got a post office, and now, uh, most the kids move away to Denver or work in the mines." A gap in the narrative so big you could float a pile of freshly hewn railroad ties through it.

Jackson, on the other hand, has it all—not just history but a modern, outside-world ambiance and a modern, outside-world story to go with it, filling in the gaps between then and now. It has impressive art museums, historic ranches, national forests and parks, wildlife to make even the most shopping-mall-blinded tourist sit up and say howdy-do. It has a long tradition of attracting artist and writer types, and lately, snowboarders and mountain climbers, all finding meaning in towering peaks, white powder, and blue-screen blue skies.

And don't forget the bars. The town of Jackson, and scattered other communities in the Hole such as Wilson and Moose, have destination bars, famous bars, bars listed on brochures and travel magazines and web sites. Bars where visitors go to just to gawk, to say they were there. Places like the Million Dollar Cowboy Bar, with its views of the antler-arched historic Town Square. Tourists go there to sit on the saddle-seated barstools, to order Cokes, and to watch the cowboys. Locals go there to mingle with strangers and have that rare experience in Wyoming: anonymity.

We were doing something akin to this during our visit to Jackson. We were seeing what life was like outside of Wyoming without having to go to the big city of Denver. At home in Laramie, many of our acquaintances live in Wyoming for one reason: they've been hired by the University of Wyoming and didn't think it through. When they have a spare afternoon, they go an hour south on dangerous roads to Ft. Collins, Colorado, for shopping. When they have a spare day or weekend, they go to Denver, two hours south, for the same. They go to those places for shopping malls, four-star restaurants, milder weather. They also go for professional theater, big time sports events, ethnic and cultural diversity. Ron and I know those things exist because we both lived many years in cities that offered those very amenities. When we miss city culture, which isn't often, we draw up our past experiences from before we moved to Wyoming, like water through a hayseed straw.

Happily, Ron and I find that Laramie has one of anything a person could need, and for us, that is enough. Many people in Laramie have no idea where Bondurant is, or Eden, or Lightning Flats. Why should they? I suppose they have no reason to know about these wide spots on the road out there in Wyoming's hinterlands. But everyone in Wyoming knows where Jackson is.

There's a bumper sticker one often sees on cars and trucks here. It says: "Wyoming is what America was." I take it to mean that America was once uncluttered, uncomplicated, and unregulated. According to that point of view, some would argue that Wyoming, with its energy boom and unpredictable future, is driving down the same highway to perdition the rest of America merged onto long ago. Maybe it's true, maybe it isn't, maybe it never was.

But the comparison still works on other scales. For example, Bondurant still is what Jackson once was. Jackson used to be a small ranching community, isolated by weather and distance from other towns in the area. Weather and distance haven't changed, but travel has. Jackson's airport has the longest runway in the state, built to accommodate the planes the jet set uses to come and go. But wealthy folks buying multi-million dollar ranches have started to figure out it is damn lonely out in a valley in the middle of thousands of acres populated mostly by cattle and coyotes. Places are going on the market, but coming off mighty slow.

But back to the Elk Horn in Bondurant. It was late afternoon when we stopped in the bar, and we were intent on reaching Jackson before the icy road through Hoback Canyon filled with darkness and deer and bighorn sheep. We were having a good time visiting with punch-line delivery man Glenn. If any modern man is now what mountain men once were, Glenn is that man. Battered cowboy hat, cuff-worn brush popper shirt and stained Carhartt vest accessorize Glenn's main feature: a large handlebar mustache that fills up half his face. A movie director could easily cast Glenn as a cowboy, a guide, or an extra of any Western type. No makeup or costumes needed: money saved.

We drank our beer and talked with Glenn about what goes on around these parts. He spends summer guiding dudes and fall guiding hunters through the local mountains and forests. In winter he looks for other work and this one coming up he hoped would be spent with a rancher acquaintance in the Laramie Valley. This acquaintance's livestock had been bothered by one or more mountain lions, which he hoped Glenn could dispatch on his behalf. Glenn was waiting to hear if this plan was going materialize. He offered to buy us another round and we reluctantly refused the drink. It was the social equivalent of turning down someone's offer of a brand new Corvette. And of all the reasons: having to get to Jackson Hole. I felt like the greenhorn in the salsa commercial who confessed to getting his spicy stuff from "New York City" (get a rope).

But leave we did, picking our way through icy dusk and deer and bighorns, and pickup trucks and SUVs and travel-trailers into Jackson Hole, past ski chalets, pricey shops and traffic lights to our own motel. I confess the days in Jackson were a blast. We spent Thanksgiving Day hiking around the Teton Mountains, walking with our dog Spike along a trail and not even needing snowshoes at the mountains' base. Later we went back to our motel, watched the Dallas Cowboys and Denver Broncos play football, drank wine, and ate sushi we'd purchased the day before from a Japanese restaurant just up the street. We had a big time, forgetting where we were for a few days, being swallowed up by snowy peaks and hardly noticing the traffic or tourists.

Eventually, though, I started to get antsy down in that deep valley. Being swallowed up by mountains that close is almost as bad as being around people who sit too near on an uncrowded bus. I prefer some space between myself and just about everything else.

When we headed back to Laramie, we made another quick stop at the Elk Horn. We hadn't spent much time there on the way in, and Ron wanted to take some pictures. It was only mid-morning on our return stop, and the bar wasn't open. We realized we should have left our phone number for Glenn, in case he did manage his winter trip to Laramie. Gloria, who owns the place, was working in the convenience store when we arrived. She pledged to get our message to Glenn, whom she expected to see later in the day. It was a slow morning, so she left the store and let us into the empty bar. She showed us the bar family photo album, including pictures of several deceased black bears slumped on stools or reclining on the bar. When local hunters kill bears or mountain lions, the custom is to bring them in, prop them up, and toast the hunter's fortunes all around.

Gloria encouraged us to come again, maybe in the summer, rent a cabin and go horseback riding. I don't have to imagine what the current snow-heavy winter has done to Bondurant or the Elk Horn. I can just go to the Bondurant town web site and click on the web cam. I can follow the links, see photos of the Elk Horn cabins, and inside of the bar. In among the images are pictures of the bar bears. They are what they were in life, but frozen on film forever.

Bondurant is what it was from its earliest days, but refreshes itself every five minutes on the web cam. I am what I will always be, non-native so just a bit out of context for the place, like a punchline without a joke. That's OK. I've always preferred the punch lines to the long complicated setups that lead into them. "Take my wife—please!" "Why the long face?" These loose punchlines are the story-telling equivalent of most of Wyoming's personality: an odd unattached range here, a hoodoo-filled basin there, people living miles from neighbors or pavement, bars out in the middle of nowhere. Wyoming has a peculiar sense of humor and lucky for crowd-hating me, it is one not everybody gets.

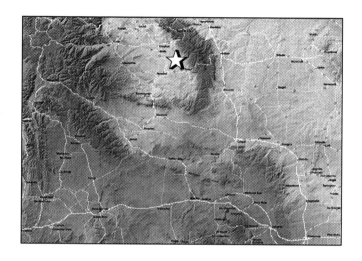

A Girl's Guide to the Universe
Rowdy's Spirits & Bait
Hyattville, Wyoming

At Rowdy's Spirits & Bait in Hyattville, walls, ceilings, and horizontal surfaces are embellished with wall art whose meaning is more than skin deep. While a few ubiquitous animal heads and bird body parts add to the ornamentation, it is the Girlie Poster that stands out as a strikingly significant portion of décor here. Girls in bikinis, pelvises thrust at distorted angles above straddling legs; girls in short shorts and tight tops tied across protruding rib cages; girls emerging Venus-like from ocean waters with perfect hair and makeup: all courtesy of beer companies with logos discreetly tucked in an unobtrusive corner of the glossy pinup. The Girlie Poster is an art form out of place in most schools, churches, and other establishments of the conventionally respectable. However, Rowdy's without the Girlie Posters would seem, well...*naked.*

About five miles up the road another kind of wall iconography draws campers, heritage tourists, and students of cultural history to the Medicine Lodge State Archaeological Site. Locals had long known about the Indian petroglyphs on the red sandstone cliffs rising above the valley floor. Then in 1969, archaeologists from the State of Wyoming began a dig that revealed evidence of human habitation in the lush Medicine Lodge Creek valley, dating back ten thousand years. The dig was led by then State of Wyoming archaeologist George Frison, now professor emeritus and retired head of the University of Wyoming Anthropology department.

There are more than six hundred images pecked or painted by prehistoric native visitors to the area, and a few others done by relatively modern settlers. The latter tend to be names and dates indicating when an individual passed through the area. The native works are thought to have been created by a steady flow of nomadic residents of the valley. Drawings by contemporary visitors to the site are frowned upon, no matter how universal the human compulsion to so mark. While folks might indulge the doodlings of a pioneer who passed this way in 1880, the musings of a local beer-soaked teenager or a tourist with a pen knife are unwelcome graffiti.

The day we stopped by Rowdy's, Dr. Frison was in town to present a talk at the site's campground, which had filled with day visitors and overnight campers for the occasion. Rowdy himself, along with the jovial Colonel Bob and a less vocal but no less communicative man named Clint, made up the bar party this July afternoon.

We'd been camping in a wilderness area in the Big Horn mountains, and had made our way slowly but not terribly far down a scenic backway (read: washed out gravel gulley) through Wyoming landscape appreciated best by those like us who see beauty in sagebrush, khaki colored soil and a vast, vast sky. We were hot and thirsty when we got to Rowdy's and took him by surprise when we ordered two cold Miller Genuine Draft beers from the cooler where we assumed the bait was also stored. Rowdy had those MGDs a long time. He mostly sold Bud and Coors—he was confident that only tourists from Michigan or some other generic "back east" location would drink anything else.

Unfortunately for us, it turns out we'd just missed Dr. Frison at the bar, where he'd stopped to spend some time with Rowdy and company, and maybe say a quick hello to the glossy Girlies on the walls and ceiling. I imagine Dr. Frison would have interesting insights about the relationship between bar owners and the ways they decorate their digs with animal parts and beer company kitsch. He and other scholars believe many prehistoric petroglyphs served a documentary purpose connected to issues of survival and belief, valuable to the extended family of native people who traveled the region.

But what purpose is served by the Girlie Poster? Is the idealistically perfect woman depicted in this imagery a goddess, there to help us know when to plant corn? The women may be licking their lips and pointing their breasts, but not to test prevailing winds or locate ground water. Girlie worship gets the worshipper no extra bounty on earth, no inside track with the goddess. However, Girlies do inspire contemplation of the relationship between airbrushes, silicone and cellulite, and maybe that's enough to think about while dodging the hot Wyoming sun in the cool quiet of Rowdy's Spirits and Bait.

Bars have long been a crossroads, a bulletin board across time and place just like the sandstone cliffs above the hospitable valley of the Medicine Lodge. Scholars have researched and written about how bars were decorated, clear back to Elizabethan England, where notices of public events crowded bar walls also festooned with religious imagery from familiar Bible stories. For various social, political and religious reasons, folks had slowed down on church-going where they had been receiving these messages, and the public houses, or "pubs," instead became a logical place for reminding people of some of the highlights of the Bible. Visitors to these alehouses might not have had Girlie posters to occupy their eyes while they ate, drank and caught up on the news of the world, but they could still reflect on the ten "Shalt Nots" from the comfort of a seventeenth century barstool.

All this musing about the meaning of wall art takes me back to my weekly childhood visits to St. Agnes Catholic Church, the parish I attended for eighteen years. St. Agnes was and is a limestone building with arched doorways and flying buttressed ceilings in the modified gothic design of 1920s American church architecture.

I recall its interior based on years of glazed-eye staring while kneeling, sitting, or standing. A marble railing ran parallel with the far wall of the church, and separated the parishioners' dark wooden pews and creaky kneelers from the spacious but defined stage that was set aside for marble saints, stately priests and adolescent altar boys. A little gate in the center of this barrier was for the priests and altar boys, the saints pretty much stayed put inside this spiritual corral. One could kneel on a marble step and lean against the railing when receiving Holy Communion or having one's throat blessed with candles on the feast of St. Blaise.

At house right in this theological theater, at the end of the railing, stood a sculpted marble Joseph, conspicuously solitary in art as he was in life, having been upstaged by his famous son, and by his wife who would soon be literally elevated above her station. House left held a seated Mary, marble cloak so like silk I swear I could have brushed it free of lint. On her lap sat a fat naked baby Jesus, a lily clutched in his little fist, eyes on his mother like she was the only thing in creation that mattered.

Far upstage in this religious tableau, a grown-up Jesus hung on a dark wooden cross probably ten feet in height. His emaciated form was excruciating to behold. The thorn-crowned head drooped lifelessly onto one shoulder, while a marble loin cloth covered part of his skeletal body. More than these features, though, I remember his hands and feet, long, thin and flat against the wood of the cross, affixed like butterflies to a spreading board.

On Sundays back then I viewed saints in marble; the rest of the time rock bands and cartoon hippies throbbed in black light on the walls and ceiling of my suburban ranch home bedroom. I spent considerable time locked away there strumming my acoustic guitar, writing angst-filled protest songs. Thumbtacked covers from *Mad* magazine hid the blue and pink butterflies of the girlie wallpaper. "Keep on Truckin'" said Mr. Natural, strolling in posture-challenging leaned back gait, platform shoed and bellbottomed.

This was the 1970s, when rock bands made record albums on vinyl, packaged with posters of questionable aesthetic value, but knowingly reflecting the self-image of teenager hippie wannabes. My father held the ladder while I tacked a 4'x6' poster of the band Chicago on my ceiling. Pink Floyd, the Guess Who, and long-haired others filled up most of the rest of the bedroom real estate. Over my desk, where I only rarely did homework, hung a Styrofoam bulletin board that was shaped like a big green frog. I'd covered it with ticket stubs from the dozens of rock concerts I attended at that stage of my life. Little was visible of the frog itself, just patches of its freckled skin between stub clusters—paper validations that I'd passed that way without my parents.

When I went to college and left home for good, the bulletin board was cast away, along with the ticket stubs documenting my adventures. How I wish I could get it back and verify which loud drug-crazed rock concerts I'd attended but forgotten, and which I'd invented but recall like I'd been on stage handling rhythm guitar myself.

Meanwhile, Rowdy—remember Rowdy? This *is* an essay about Rowdy—had his own iconic truths, presented in a pictogram on the flip side of his Spirits &

Bait business card. After we'd had a beer or two he presented it to Ron and me and could barely contain his gloating as he and Colonel Bob tried to coach us through unraveling the riddle.

Here's what's on the card: Typed across the top when held horizontally is the text "If You Know Your Baseball." Below those words are four hand drawn pictures, to be read from left to right. The images are these: a clock, its long hand on the five, its short hand on the four; an upside down bottle, dispensing a drop of liquid into a small glass below it; a woman in a bra with only one cup, leaving the other breast uncovered; a toilet with the lid open.

After displaying humiliating stupidity, we stumbled or were pushed into the correct interpretation by the prompting of Rowdy, Colonel Bob, and the quieter Clint. I'm not going to give you the answer here. Rowdy would be too disappointed. How would he torment future customers who'd always thought they were fairly bright, before they met him?

Trying to find the right answer in a mystery inscrutable to some but obvious to others reminds me how both frustrating and revealing interpreting images can be. Take those Medicine Lodge pictographs and petroglyphs. If only nomadic native people would have left some written crib sheet explaining what they meant by the ghastly and frightening, by the whimsical, by the literal. We could then understand them as certainly as we understand the Girlie Poster, the Ten Commandments, the Guess Who, or the agony of the Crucifixion. Unfortunately, the pictures stored in our own memories have no rubric that I'm aware of. What symbolic archeological dig can help us explain ourselves to ourselves? If we stare into ourselves as long and intently as some of Rowdy's Girlies stare at one another across the bar, perhaps we'd come up with some answers. Or maybe we'd just order a six pack of cold beer and some bait to go. We'd pack a picnic and fish by moonlight, deciphering life's seasons beneath the stars.

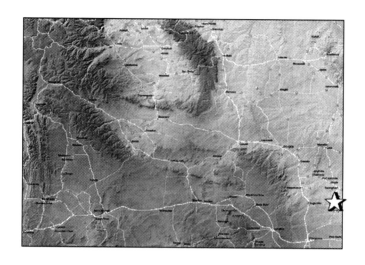

Bar Theater 101
Long Branch Saloon
Hawk Springs, Wyoming

Act 1 Scene 1
Exterior:

Mid-afternoon on an unseasonably warm mid-March day in Hawk Springs, in southeast Wyoming, just a handful of miles from the Nebraska border.

A man and a woman emerge from a car, a mid 1990s, small green SUV, which they've just parked in the shade. They stretch a bit from having made an apparently long but leisurely trip. They wear blue jeans and long-sleeved shirts, but no jackets. They approach the front door of the Long Branch Saloon. Its Western façade and wooden sidewalk porch are authentically—not Hollywood—dusty. With a wave to the little white dog waiting in the car, they enter the building.

Act 1 Scene 2
Interior:

A barroom, square in shape, with the bar running along the right hand wall, as seen from the front entrance. Barstools are occupied by a couple who look to be in their sixties. A man in his twenties hovers over another stool, using the telephone. Two women in their thirties tend bar. All are dressed in jeans and T-shirts or sweaters. Behind the bar, glass shelves hold a hodgepodge of liquor bottles. Neon bar lights glitter against brown and green glass. At the near end of the bar is a doorway that opens onto a small store. At the far end of the bar another door leads to a kitchen. Straight back from the door, the sign over a large open doorway leading to a restaurant says "Long Branch." The restaurant is empty at this time of the afternoon but will be busy later. In the center of the room a game of pool is being played briskly and with concentration by two men, one middle aged, the other a bit older. Scattered around the pool table are several tables and chairs, occupied variously by groups of young men and older couples. A jukebox crowds one corner of the pool table and booms a contemporary hit country tune.

The man and woman (call them Ron and Julianne) take two barstools, near the couple but with one intervening stool.

Bartender One: What can I get you?

Ron: Two Miller Genuine Drafts.

Bartender One: That'll be five dollars.

Julianne (to Ron): I think this is going to be a great spot on the Bar Tour.

And so on and so on. You get the picture. Scenes in bars, when reported accurately (by which I mean linearly) can seem pretty dull. But after spending lots of time in bars, one understands that bar time is not linear, no matter what the clock face may show. Like in Anton Chekhov's play *The Cherry Orchard*, time plunks from an unseen harp out onto the bar in little discrete notes, some whole, some quarter, in various keys and time signatures. One can pick up these notes of time and nibble on them between drinks, or leave them lying on the floor to roll or be kicked about by careless feet. Partners can aim and flick them back and forth through goal-post fingers. Sometimes they can be dropped into jukeboxes or pool tables. Rarely do they advise when to go home.

As you've just seen from the above metaphor, writers use various literary devices to describe events that constitute time passing in, for example, a bar somewhere in Wyoming. These devices are used to prevent one-damn-thing-after-another storytelling and to create, instead, something interesting.

Here's an example of one device, called narrative summary. It is best used in short bursts in order to avoid the method described above, because it takes as long to describe action as the action itself takes to unfold:

A man enters the front door of the bar and lets it slam behind him. As his eyes adjust to the lower illumination indoors, several men at a corner table glance his way, and then exchange looks among themselves. The man pauses a moment and then makes his way through the casually arranged tables, past the pool table, and leans against the wall a couple feet from the table where the men are seated.

Another technique is flashback. This tool is useful after the scene setting established in the last example, and opens up the story to elements taking place outside the bar:

As the cold bubbly beer glides down his throat he thinks of his pioneer great-grandfather, who in the late nineteenth century traveled on an emigrant trail near this spot on his way West. What Grampy would have given for a ready supply of something other than alkaline creek water (insert a visual device here in which time ripples backwards and reveals a Conestoga wagon perched above a creek bed, driven by a young Grampy in red kerchief and greasy hat).

Then there is the question of handling dialog in bar scene réportage. The idea here is not to transcribe big long blocks of pointless conversation, but to try to establish mood and character through representative speech. It could go like this:

As the men play pool, the first man says, "Side pocket."

"Ughnn," the second man replies, nodding.

"Click," says the eight ball to the side pocket.

"Go again?" says the first man.

"Ughnn," the second man replies again, dropping quarters into the slotted slide lever at the end of the table.

Alas, literary devices alone do not a story make. What's really needed is plot, with exposition, complication, climax, false resolution and final resolution. This essay is part of a larger story about rural bars situated throughout the state of Wyoming. Here is the grand design of the full story, in a bar nutshell:

Title: *Jukeboxes & Jackalopes: A Wyoming Bar Journey.*

Exposition: All around the state stand little tiny towns with one bar or maybe the bar is the entire town. The bars serve as public living rooms for folks who live or work in the area.

Complication: As people looking for work leave rural areas, tiny towns evaporate from the landscape. This trend is documented nationwide, and Wyoming seems to be following suit. How will these little towns, and their little bars, survive?

Climax: Two strangers pop into a bar and explain that they are on a bar tour of Wyoming. Everyone within hearing distance in the particular bar suggests more destinations for the tour. Soon a long list of really great bars is inventoried, a web site is developed, a book plan is hatched, and lots of people look forward to reading about and seeing photographs of the places they've loved or would love to explore.

False Resolution: Farms, ranches, small towns— none create an economic mattress that can comfort and support residents. Those residents leave for bigger towns where there are other places to gather besides bars. Sure, a few bars remain open and convert to exotic dance clubs, to accommodate the tastes of temporary residents who work in the energy industry. In twenty years all these places will be boarded up, and the few remaining rural residents, isolated from human contact, will melt down in front of their television sets at home, like butter into popcorn.

Resolution: As seen through the eyes of the bar tourists, who realize no public venue better reflects life around this state. Like species of mice or toads known only to exist in one inconvenient spot, rural bars are a product of the environment that nurtures them and if they die, the cycle of life around them is changed. Wyoming residents become social environmentalists and active stewards of their small communities, which they won't allow to be bulldozed by time or progress.

That story tells the tale of the Wyoming bar tour in a rather tidy way. And it actually rather works for describing this literary endeavor. But stories in each individual bar don't follow traditional structure, and that is as true for the Long Branch as for any other. Bar stories overlap and intersect like storylines in a long running soap opera.

"Jack" and "Hope" could have just gotten married last month while skydiving, but if you missed that episode you would never understand why next month they plan to skydive while signing their divorce papers. You have to watch for awhile before you are in the know.

Because bar action ebbs and flows, it can be thought of in terms of a literary entity called French scenes. In a stage play, a new French scene begins every time a character enters or leaves the action. Bar action is like a never ending play. The busier the bar, the more often people come and go and thus subtly affect the mood of the other patrons.

Scene i: Boisterous people having a good time exit a bar and take a little bubble of laughter-filled air with them.

Scene ii: The drunk at the end of the bar finally goes home and leaves everyone else with a nagging sense of concern about the drunk's prospects for getting there safely.

Scene iii: In walk a pair of men who've just gotten off a local lake and have parked their truck, boat trailer and boat in the lot. Their conversation with the bartender about weather and fishing luck absorb the interest of everyone on nearby stools.

Scene iv: Eventually the pool players leave, and patrons who are strangers in the bar have lost the place to focus their stares and turn instead to one another. They order large burgers from the menu and another beer.

Ideally, each French scene not only advances the plot, it tells you a bit more about the characters, and especially illuminates the protagonist. But first, just who is the protagonist of this tale?

The protagonist of this bar story is the Long Branch itself. Since protagonists are characters that one roots for, first we have to know who that character is. Writers establish characters in all sorts of ways: descriptions of age, education, ethnicity, physical appearance, clothing style, manner of movement and speech. Bars may be described in similar terms. Here's a description of the Long Branch crafted with the hope that readers will come to understand something about the place and care about it, just a little bit.

The Long Branch is a combination bar/restaurant/ store that comprises most of the town of Hawk Springs. It has stood near the intersection of U.S. 85 and Road 182 in Goshen County long enough to have seen its fair share of highway repaving operations thunder past its door. If the Long Branch could talk it would twang; if it could eat, steak would be on the plate; if it could marry, a grain elevator would be its mate. For the Long Branch stands in extreme eastern Wyoming, east of Chugwater, east of Goshen Hole, nearly to Nebraska, where most people who make their living off the land are farmers, not ranchers.

The Long Branch likes pheasant hunting and harvests, thunderstorms and rainbows, University of Nebraska football and Chadron State baseball. Its friends are fishermen, bikers on their way to the Sturgis motorcycle rally, and folks up and down Wyoming's east coast taking Sunday drives past reservoirs and rivers.

As just demonstrated, writers often anthropomorphize non-humans in stories to create literary characters. Look at the Mississippi River in Mark Twain's *Huckleberry Finn.* If ever there were a force capable of effecting change or of being loved, hated and feared, it's that river. The Long Branch may not be capable of prompting a young boy to contemplate freedom and self-determination, but it does have a talent for bringing people together and encouraging conversation between strangers. It can prompt average writers to attempt literary feats beyond their talents. It can inspire dramas as recorded below: the striking up of a friendship.

Act I Scene 3

Interior, same as before. Ron and Julianne are still seated at the bar in the Long Branch. Ron is on the far end, Julianne to his right, an empty stool is to her right, then a woman, then to the woman's right, that woman's husband. All four sip bottled beer.

Julianne to the woman: Do you all live near here?

Woman: No, we're just out for a drive. We're on our way to visit our daughter in Nebraska.

Ron: We're from Laramie. We're trying to visit all the little bars in Wyoming.

Woman: That sounds fun. Do you know about Hartville?

Ron: Isn't that up on Guernsey Reservoir?

Woman: Yes, that's it. We have the Mercantile there, and we're working on restoring it.

Julianne: Great! We'll have to make sure to come up. What all are you doing to it?

Man: We're pretty much redoing it all inside.

Ron: We've been up by there before. It's by Sunrise, isn't it?

Man: Yep.

Julianne (to Ron): Didn't we drive by there when we were camping last summer?

Bartender (to group): Can I bring you all something?

Woman (to Bartender, Ron and Julianne): No, thanks. We have to head out now, but it was nice to meet you all.

And so on. No flashbacks, no dramatic dialog, not much character reveal. Just a conversation in a bar. Bars are theater where customers are both actors and audience. If one spends too much time as audience, one never strikes up friendships and gets invited on to other places, where new bar stories are waiting to be lived and written.

Heard from offstage: a long lingering brush of a string from an unseen harp. It fills the air and invites all who hear it to say hello to the strangers seated next to them, and use time the best way they can.

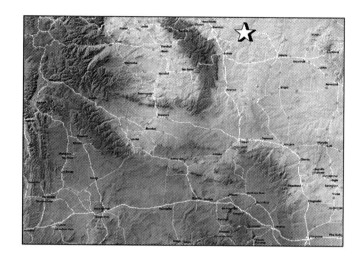

I'll Have a Town, Please
Leiterville Country Club/Joe's Place
Leiter, Wyoming

A Wyoming Bar Journey

Leiter is like many Wyoming towns: It has its own dot on the highway map, which is how you know it exists. When you get there you'll see just one or two structures, hardly qualifying as a town by most definitions, unless you are in Wyoming where big is really big and small is really small. The main structure in tiny Leiter is the Leiterville Country Club. The one-story rambler is composed of a café in the front of the building, a post office in the side wing, and a bar known as Joe's Place in the rear of the building, all accessible from the two front doors or from another door leading off an umbrella-tabled patio. Nearby stands the residence of the Country Club's owner, Martha, and a few motel rooms with beds and warm showers.

We learned about the place from some Laramie friends, Brian and Dana. They'd stopped a few summers back after roughing it tent camping in the Big Horn Mountains. They needed some good food, cold beer, a real washroom, and conversation with somebody other than each other. They'd enjoyed the marvels at the Leiterville Country Club and thought we would, too. You don't forget a good watering hole, even when it is clear across the state.

On this particular bright hot Wyoming July afternoon, skinny shadows cast by the high sun tried to hide under the few cars parked outside the Leiterville Country Club. On a scorcher like this we expected the bar to be filled with regular daytime customers, but when we walked into the low-ceilinged, antique-dotted Country Club we were surprised to discover that all the customers were up front in the café, and the bar in back was empty.

Our notion of what to expect on this bar tour was upended by the vision of groups of people sitting around munching club sandwiches and drinking iced tea by the pitcher. What kind of bar is Joe's Place, we wondered, where people eschew it in favor of a few ferns and touches of country décor in a café?

We could see Joe's Place promised comfort and good times. Large mounted animal heads, a full-body black bear, a pile of books and a TV/VCR facing a recliner accessorized the ordinary bar outfit of pool table and barstools. Instead of sitting alone in the bar like a couple anti-social alcoholics, we realized we'd need to join the crowd in the front room.

As lead talker in this project I felt stymied. In a bar it is very easy to strike up conversations and get a feel for the mood and tone of a place. A jocular bartender, an old timey customer, a silent problem drinker on the last stool: all were familiar characters in bar tour theater, until now. Here we faced ranching folks and travelers eating and drinking at separate tables and booths, engaging in minimal intra-table conversation. Inter-table conversation was not likely.

We ordered sandwiches from the short menu but with beer instead of tea, just to keep our heads in the game. Sipping beer and gobbling a Reuben properly prepared with dripping Thousand Island dressing, I looked around the room to prospect for local color. Like all writers worth their weight in yellow pads, I was prepared to eavesdrop for a good story.

One table looked interesting: a round four-top peopled by three middle-aged men in jeans who appeared to work for a living, finishing lunch with cigarettes and a refill of iced tea. They were a bit far away for me to get a very good listen, but I could hear a few words like "wells" and "drilling" and "energy."

I thought back to our arrival, when we had asked our waitress about motel rooms advertised by a sign outside. We'd considered surrendering to the low elevation furnace of northern Wyoming and staying a night in Leiter, using it as a jumping off spot for some other nearby bars we planned to tour. But we were told the rooms were full up—workers from the coal bed methane patch would occupy them for the foreseeable future.

The identity of the men seated at the four-top took shape like genies from the smoke of that earlier information: I understood now that they were employees of the energy company having a bit of a late lunch. They were just a few of a large army of working energy company men and women marching through Wyoming.

An outfit called Galaxy Energy Corporation has contracted with another outfit called Continental Industries to run its drilling operation in northern Wyoming. They are drilling holes in the ground from which they'll release methane gas from deep in the coal beds that lie in vast underground deposits in this part of the state.

The particulars of the energy industry in Wyoming are complex and good fuel for conversations around many a local bar. The upshot is that the energy companies pay millions to the state in severance taxes because they take away, or "sever," a commodity from the place they found it. Some folks argue that they don't pay enough, and that the big companies don't do enough to support the local areas where they work, and that they have undue influence on our state and local governments. Other folks worry about the effects of drilling on wildlife such as antelope and sage grouse, and aesthetic aspects of the landscape made less beautiful by oil rigs and potentially contaminated groundwater.

On the other hand, some point out that without the money paid by these big companies, Wyoming would likely have to implement a state sales tax which, with so few taxpayers, would barely finance our roads, schools, and other essential government services. Further, the nation would also be in worse shape than it currently is for meeting its energy needs without robust extraction activity in places with oil and minerals to spare. Finally, they keep the doors of a little business like this swinging.

Regardless of how one feels about the energy industry, it does exist, and its workers do make a big impact when there is an energy boom. Like this day in Leiter, when we tried to find a motel room and couldn't. In fact, that turned out to be a theme in many Wyoming locations where they "have methane in." However, the workers did give us a good topic of conversation once we found somebody to talk to. We knew that our loquacious Laramie friends, Brian and Dana, had found somebody to converse with here, and we were determined to do the same. As we paid our bill we mentioned to our waitress, Jill, that we were on a bar tour of Wyoming and we wanted to know if we could take some pictures in the Leiterville Country Club. When she learned we were from Laramie, she introduced us to her mother, Martha. They opened up like a fresh book of matches, bursting with information in short bright flares.

Turns out that Martha has owned the place for about ten years. The family used to live in Laramie, in a house about three blocks from where we live now. They moved away thirty years ago. They still have a cabin in the Snowy Range Mountains west of Laramie, though they don't go there much anymore. Martha doesn't have many friends left in Laramie, because most have died or moved away, but she offers that she remembers meeting a couple from Laramie named Brian and Dana, who stopped into the Country Club once. (She doesn't seem surprised to learn we know them, too.) Martha used to own a dress shop in Buffalo, and thought maybe knew about it.

One of Martha's friends "has" Aladdin, which means she owns the bar/café/store/motel that comprises that town northeast of Leiter, so therefore she "owns" the town. Aladdin was named for the character in *The Arabian Nights*, in order to conjure images of good luck and riches in this spot where the town founder had hoped to establish a railroad. Martha doesn't know what all her friend sells in the store because in the years Martha's friend has had it, Martha's never had time to visit, nor has she ever seen some of Wyoming's most famous tourist spots, such as Devil's Tower. She's too busy being almost the sole chef and manager of the Leiterville Country Club, with some help from Jill and a few area women who pitch in when somebody in Buffalo wants to hold a holiday party, or when there is an event to cater. Most of her regular customers are nearby ranching people or folks from Buffalo. The men from the energy company just come and go. They don't ever stay long, so they are hard to get to know.

We wondered if the transient nature of the community around Leiter was the cause of the lack of people in Joe's Place on this hot afternoon that seemed made for beer drinking. Do strangers in the motel and café mean fewer friends in the bar? Or were we just over thinking it, making too much of the events of one visit? At any rate, the local rural residents around here have frequented the place since Joe Leiter founded it. But others, like seasonal insects, come and go when conditions are right. As Dorothy observed of Oz, "People come and go so quickly here." Indeed they do, be they energy workers, tourists, or ramblers on bar tours of Wyoming.

A Wyoming Bar Journey

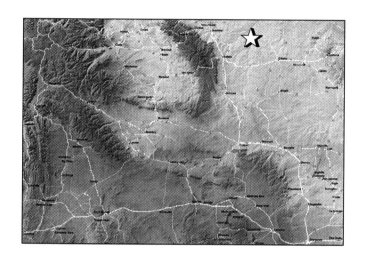

It All Comes out of a Bottle
The Arvada Saloon
Arvada, Wyoming

A Wyoming Bar Journey

On a side road off Wyoming 14, meandering southeast off I-90, at the confluence of Crazy Woman and Wildhorse Creeks and the Powder River, stands the village of Arvada. A few buildings and houses hunker on a hillside. Near the road through town a wind-stripped wooden structure with a false Western façade is signed "The." Fortunately for anyone traveling by this spot where the paved road through town turns to gravel, "The" is identifiable as a bar by the circa 1970 Hamm's Beer sign on the frame façade that juts up above the front porch like a snow fence. The smaller notices for Coors Light and Miller Genuine Draft complete the identity check. "The" is in fact the Arvada Bar, the middle syllable pronounced with a long "a," not a hoity-toity extended pinky "ah" like the Denver suburb of the same name.

Two cars are in the lot. One is an early 1990s Dodge, parked right outside the front door, a blue handicapped tag hooked over the rearview mirror although no parking spots are delineated here, handicapped or otherwise. A sticker on its back bumper declares "Need Advice? Ask God!" The other vehicle is a late model silver PT Cruiser with eyes-open-wide headlights and bulbous fenders. Its design evokes an earlier time—not of the West, but perhaps of Germany between the wars, though most of drivers of this model are too young to recall the Maginot Line. This Cruiser's side door sports a cartoon Betty Boop, also popular in the 1930s. Betty signals us that this car belongs to a bona fide Avon lady, whose name (Dana) and phone number are painted at the tip of Betty's manicured fingernails.

A third vehicle at rest in some nearby shrubbery looks like its owner came to the bar long ago and forgot to leave. It is a half-ton pickup truck, the color of dust and rust, with a bumper sticker on its front windshield advertising the Mint Bar in Sheridan, about seventy miles northwest of here at the foot of the Big Horn Mountains. When and how the truck's owners came by that bumper sticker is a question, since the truck is vintage 1920s and looks no longer ambulatory. In fact, its decaying body would now test the powers of even the best collision and repair shop in Sheridan County.

The Arvada Bar had been recommended to us by the folks at the Leiterville Country Club, who thought we'd like to see what had lately turned in to a hoppin' little spot, especially on Friday nights. But this was a Tuesday afternoon, so we were going to see the place before company came. On this day a sprawling border collie snoozed on the cool floor, herding tiles in his sleep. A man and young boy perched on high barstools and munched pizza slices. The most loyal customers, who never gave the bartender any grief, lined the walls above arm's reach. If this were Britain, the dusty stuffed bison, deer and trout would have lost count of how many times they'd heard a punctual, "Time, please gentlemen" and seen the crowd shuffle out the door and the lights go out.

The Arvada Bar is tended by a sandy haired woman of middle age. She lives a few miles away in a town aptly named Recluse, a place even less likely to attract casual tourists than Arvada. She drives the PT Cruiser, and as we deduced, sells Avon. Of course, Avon products are touted to make their users look and feel younger. They are a balm against dilating pores, darkening shadows, and drooping dewlaps.

What better place to find a peddler of bottled miracles than in the Arvada Bar? After all, there is a local precedent for miraculous, or at least astounding, goings-on. Arvada once had an artesian well whose water was forced out of the ground by natural gas. Locals are said to have astounded tourists by lighting a match near the water, igniting the gas, and then drinking the flaming water.

Today some bottled water companies sell water labeled as artesian, evoking images of toga-clad nymphs lolling around a pool, sipping the earth's first tears. Labels picturing flaming drinking water wouldn't sell as well to today's consumers. Too reminiscent of Lake Erie in the 1970s.

To say this is a place that time forgot, or that it is a place right out of the old West, would be to rely on clichés, but in this case there's no reason to reinvent the wheel of descriptive language. It is quintessentially both of those things because of its location on a road off a highway—off a highway.

The function of places is shaped by their surroundings: resorts on big lakes offer water recreation; restaurants in cattle country offer steaks; bars on the highway offer gasoline and maps. The mineral-laden rocky bluffs, the shot-out road signs, the gravel road that leads out of town and the paved one that leads in, shape the Arvada Bar, social center to this rural community.

From the exterior, the Arvada Bar looks tired. Central casting should send over a few tumbleweeds and cowboys to complete the look. Dana's Avon products could never contain enough vitamins or collagen to reanimate the rusted out pickup truck in the lot, or recharge the fluorescent beer signs in the window. But who needs youth in a bottle when the real thing is a topic of discussion right there?

The conversation on the afternoon of our visit centered on the young people of Arvada, specifically, the six male and eight female students who attended the K-6 elementary school in town. The students have two teachers among them, and one of them was right here in the bar on this summer afternoon.

This teacher enjoyed telling us about her students. They would go on to junior high seven miles away at the combined Arvada-Clearmont Junior High, which boasted seventeen students and one teacher. Their next stop would be to the six teachers at Arvada-Clearmont High School, who would prepare just under fifty students for the future, very possibly at the University of Wyoming. The teacher and another woman who'd joined her were not much interested in our bar tour, but they wanted to know more about what I'd disclosed was my day job: University of Wyoming English teacher.

We chatted for awhile about the No Child Left Behind Act, the federal government's plan to make schools accountable for the performance of their students. The venom she didn't spit at this law, which she felt was unsuited for rural schools such as hers, was saved for Wyoming's testing system, which she also seemed to feel didn't work terribly well.

Though her students had done well in testing, especially in math, she was concerned about their writing ability, and whether they would be prepared for what they'd face at UW. She talked about teachers' concerted efforts to instruct students to write five paragraph themes: the very formula UW writing teachers encourage our students to move beyond. I told her we help students to think of writing as a way to ask questions and solve problems, rather than a way to introduce points of rhetoric like required elements in a gymnastics routine. Many of our students have come to believe writing is like taking words and adding enough water to grow an introductory paragraph that starts "Since the beginning of time, man has always...". That introduction will then grow into an essay, they hope, like a prose Chia Pet.

I'm not sure if talking to me about this topic was illuminating for the local teacher, but it certainly was for me. If learning more about Wyoming's rural life was one goal of the bar tour, seeing the environments that shape my students' lives was a marvelous bonus. Like me, many UW faculty members originally came from larger metropolitan areas. It is easy for us to think of the 28,000 people in Laramie as comprising a very small town. But by the measure of most Wyoming places, Laramie is the "big city."

Students coming from a town with ten kids in the school react in one of several ways to the crowds, the traffic, and the entertainment—both legal and illegal. Some fancy themselves liberated: bingeing at all-night house parties and sleeping through class the next day is possible when one is anonymous, when there are more people in an Introduction to Biology class than in one's home town. Other students seem unchanged and doggedly march toward the future of sober employment by studying a practical major. They barely seem to notice the social change raging around them, and believe *a priori* that environmentalists are whacko and that the GOP is the only political party worth voting for.

A third bunch of students appear to wilt when they arrive in the big town of Laramie. They devalue their background and the non-academic literacies they've attained through seventeen years of rural or small town life. When asked where they are from, they almost always attach the identifier "Wyoming" to the name of their town, as if no UW professor would otherwise have heard of Dubois or Pinedale, Torrington or Gillette. But of course we have, because those young college students eventually grow into older more experienced very smart college students, who go on to make a name for the towns that helped shape them.

The Arvada school teacher, her friend, Dana the bartender, and the two us of solved many of the problems of Wyoming and the world on that afternoon in the bar. It was time to say goodbye to these new friends, the border collie, and the stuffed heads at ease on the walls.

As we got ready to leave and make the turn onto the paved road from whence we came, I fingered the bar souvenirs Dana had found for us. A small calendar with a sticky back, so we'd always remember where we were on the past-present-future continuum, and a Bic pen with the bar's name on it, so we could leave someone a note in case we lost our way. No wrinkle-concealing Avon products though. For us, youth and age come out of life's spigot together, like natural gas and water, impossible to extinguish without first lighting a nice big distilling flame.

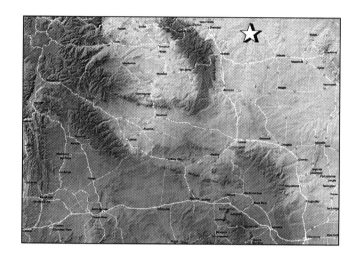

The Horse of a Different Color
Spotted Horse Saloon
Spotted Horse, Wyoming

Reared up on hind legs, a black horse with white spots balances a platter-shaped sign on one upraised hoof. The sign reads "Spotted Horse." The fifteen-foot tall fiberglass critter is indeed a spotted horse, the place it heralds is a bar called Spotted Horse, the bar comprises the entire town of Spotted Horse (Population 2), and all of it is named for a long-deceased Indian Chief called, predictably, Spotted Horse. This is a literal land, where a tall cottonwood at the corner of the small white building means shade, and a shadow under the back porch means rattlesnake shelter. Wide open grasslands mean ranches and dry stream beds in summer, and troughs for run-off the next spring. Natural gas under all of it means good economic times in northeast Wyoming, where an energy boom fueled by coal bed methane drilling brings business to tiny Spotted Horse.

Light but regular traffic vrooms past Spotted Horse on two-lane Interstate 14/16, kicking up road dust. Energy workers in company-issued white pickup trucks ping pong from their trailer homes in Gillette to the drilling rigs dotting the prairie. Other traffic has a more recreational pastime in view. Aiming west on this highway, tourists make their way across the Big Horn Mountains, past Cody, and on into Yellowstone National Park. Famous mountains and lakes, dramatic geysers, and wildlife large enough to be spotted through a windshield provide unambiguous beauty. But in this part of the state crossed by Burlington Northern Railroad tracks and creeks named Bitter and Wildcat, the low-elevation desert scenery is understated, and goes unappreciated by many observers.

Ron and I had already stopped in Leiter and Arvada that day of the bar tour, so we decided to bypass Spotted Horse in favor of getting to the area where we'd planned to camp for the night. But as we approached Spotted Horse, we could see storm clouds building southeast toward Gillette and over the Thunder Basin National Grasslands, where we planned to camp. Lightning bolts were visible for miles with few hills to obscure our view of their stabs at the earth. I had an idea of what electricity would look like if power cords were see-through. I also had an idea our plan for camping wasn't looking so inviting in this weather. Then I spotted that fifteen foot fiberglass horse, and it was as if that upraised hoof held a personal invitation on its oversized platter. Camping could wait.

Some bars look inviting from the outside, with glowing beer signs and wide porches coaxing customers off the road. This place looked like an establishment where fights were common among friends, but strangers weren't worth the effort. We'd already pulled into the parking lot and would have felt self-conscious chickening out and turning back onto the highway. We were like race car drivers, figuratively past the commitment cones marking the entrance to pit road. So we took a deep breath, and in our tourist T-shirts and car-rumpled shorts, pulled open the metal-grilled screen door and stepped into the dimly cluttered Spotted Horse Saloon.

"Leiterville Country Club!?" exclaimed the bartender, with a Price-is-Right come on down smile. "Where'd you get that?"

I realized I was wearing the sun visor that advertised the Leiterville Country Club, about twenty-five miles up the road. Martha and Jill had given it to us earlier that day, and I wore it proudly. We made our way past the Spotted Horse pool table and assorted dusty big game trophy mounts to the bar. It turns out that sun visor was better than any secret handshake or amulet, because it made us more insider than total stranger, and centered the bar conversation on us, at least long enough to settle in on barstools and explain that we were on a bar tour of Wyoming. We asked if there was a bar artifact, such as a book of matches or a coaster, that we could add to our growing trinket collection.

The bartender, whose name was Jerome, paced back and forth behind the bar rustling through boxes and rummaging behind liquor decanters, searching for a Spotted Horse souvenir.

"I ordered beer cozies a month ago and they still aren't here," he grumbled. Finally he produced a round red token, like a smooth poker chip, printed with the Spotted Horse name and promising a free beer if redeemed. Mission accomplished, he and we settled back into the friendly banter we'd interrupted.

An English couple named Nick and Fiona were wrapping up their afternoon at the bar. Their Wyoming visit was more of a saturation tour, of which bar hopping was only a portion. International tourists don't usually find their way to such out of the way spots as this, and we admired their gumption for embracing the unknown. They sat at a tall table near a window drinking pale American beer, taking shelter from a July afternoon that was close to a hundred degrees, hotter than any place in Britain.

Through that same window we watched a silver PT Cruiser pull into the parking lot and who should enter the bar but Dana, the bartender from Arvada, on her way to a quiet evening at home in the aptly named town of Recluse. Dana greeted us and the other folks there and mentioned that she was about to go to jail. Not the county jail, but jail for a day in Sheridan, to raise money for the Muscular Dystrophy Association in their annual fund drive. Jerome obligingly provided bailout money to keep her incarceration brief. Dana wanted to be out of jail in plenty of time to get to the bead shop in Sheridan before it closed at six-thirty p.m.

Another member of this chummy party was local ranch woman, who was having a cool drink and waiting for her husband to arrive. His tardiness was a perfect opportunity to talk about him, and so she explained to Jerome and the rest of us that they were planning to fashion an outdoor awning system for the house to give it a bit more shade in this treeless prairie. But her husband was in charge of the design and building and she wasn't real sure when the job would be done, so she thought she'd have to take matters into her own hands.

"He told me when we got married not to buy a laundry hamper because he'd design me one. That was thirty-two years ago."

As they all chatted about awnings and beads and rattlesnakes, we began taking stock of the knick knacks on the back bar and environs. There were the expected items like Western memorabilia and beer company trinkets. There were photographs of people and places, some dating back generations. Among the rubble of kitsch was an antique doll Jerome had just purchased in Keystone, South Dakota. He and Dana examined her frozen features and starched outfit. "The only thing she's missing is her hat," Jerome noted regretfully.

About this time, my impression of the bar as a rough and tumble place evaporated. I wanted to tell Jerome and company all about my own collections: salt and pepper sets; troll dolls; books; musical instruments, LPs on vinyl. But I was so fascinated by this most unexpected of bar conversations I couldn't find the words to interrupt. Instead I listened, while Jerome, in his red white & blue ball cap, chatted with Dana about a Barbie outfit she was crocheting and about the various antique shops in the Black Hills area.

The Black Hills are one of my favorite spots in Wyoming. On the South Dakota side they are an especially popular destination, particularly in the summer as people pour in to visit Mt. Rushmore or to attend the Harley Davidson Motorcycle Rally in Sturgis each August. Numerous tunnels cut through the mountains allow the highway to slip through rock like thread through a needle. The tunnels are designed to move traffic, but they do invite a hazard as each tunnel opens closer and closer to views of Mt. Rushmore and its dynamite-carved faces of famous presidents.

An exasperated Jerome described some near misses with people stopped at the mouths of tunnels to photograph the attraction. "I wish they'd stop taking pictures of Mt. Rushmore!" he declared—futilely I'm afraid.

Jerome served us our first soft-drinks of the bar tour, then he showed us all a framed photograph of a wedding party in which he'd taken part as a small boy. The wedding was fifty years ago, and recently there'd been an anniversary party thrown by the family, who still lived in the area of North Dakota where Jerome grew up. Everyone at the anniversary gathering who'd been in the wedding party posed for an updated group photo. Only a man named Elmer was no longer around.

These homey conversations were interrupted occasionally by coal bed methane workers stopping in at the end of their shifts for six-packs of Pepsi and a couple hot dogs to go. Jerome gave each a quick nod when they approached the bar to order. I wondered how local people felt about all the transient oil and gas workers filling the countryside as of late. The impacts of all this drilling are numerous, from artesian wells drying up, to hay meadows flooding with salinated water, to excessive mosquitoes spawning in standing ground water discharged from methane company wells. The mosquitoes carry West Nile virus, which they spread to humans and wildlife including sage grouse, which partially accounts for the recent drop in that population.

On the other hand, these workers and the economic boom they represent make a huge difference for local businesses. But when oil and gas workers stopped in for provisions after their shift, they didn't seem to relax and be part of the crowd like the regulars did, or even like the English tourists or we did. Their to-go orders signaled that to them, Spotted Horse wasn't a social club: it was a convenience store. I asked Colleen, who operates the bar with Jerome and makes up the other half of Population 2, if that lack of social connection bothered the regulars.

"Please make sure you let people know how important the workers are to us," Colleen emphatically replied. "They're the ones that keep our doors open."

If it is true that the energy boom keeps little bars around Wyoming in operation, then I am for it. It is up to us more permanent Wyoming folks to make sure the boom doesn't get out of hand, keeping us going in the short run but burning us out over time. I hope places like Spotted Horse will always rear friskily up on hind legs and invite customers new and old in off the road.

Spotted Horse is a paradoxical place, where things are not what they seem. The bar looks rough on the outside, but houses antique-doll loving bartenders who become worked up when they can't find souvenirs for customers. The village sits on land that look great for ranching, but also harbors oil and gas that when extracted can change the land for a long time, and not often for the better. Spotted Horse shows up on the map, even though the post office that put it there closed years ago.

The skies above Spotted Horse filled with spiraling cumulus clouds that afternoon after we left the bar, and showed all the signs of a flash flood in the making. We opted out of camping in the Thunder Basin, and were lucky to find a room in a 6-holer motel on a reservoir in a nearby state park called Keyhole. We dragged two motel chairs out of our room and onto the strip of concrete in front of our door. From there, we gazed across the reservoir to the south as mammoth thunderheads shot lighting to the ground and spawned tornadoes over the distant grasslands. The fiberglass Spotted Horse stood his ground on two feet against the lash of horizontal rain. He'd seen it all before and knew that sometimes things were exactly what they seemed.

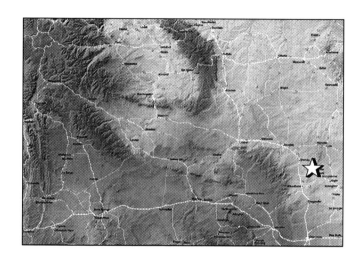

Ghosts of Towns
Miners Bar
Hartville, Wyoming

The history of Platte County, Wyoming, is engraved in the walls and ceiling of the Miners Bar in Hartville. It is upholstered into the bar's furnishings, chinked into its architecture, stacked up in its jukebox, and stowed in dusty boxes in the building's dark basement. Some of the history is of the quantifiable sort that could be counted out on an abacus or recorded in a book, like the dates when pioneers traveled through and left wagon ruts and signatures in the area's soft limestone; like the year when the bar was built to accommodate miners and stockmen; and like the moment when the neighboring Sunrise Mine finally shut down, shutting down the town of Sunrise with it.

In an area where so many families have created these stories for generations, it is difficult to draw a line between the measurable sort of history that describes past events, and the sort that reveals the personal background of individuals. So many people one meets in this county, and in Goshen County to the east, are fourth, fifth, sixth, or seventh generation Wyoming residents. Not just residents of Wyoming as a whole, but residents of this particular low elevation, sand colored, bright sky-ed place. The longer newcomers spend in this area, the more likely they are to find out that the folks they just had a nice chat with in line at the grocery store are the parents or children or grandparents of somebody they met in line someplace else an hour earlier. One needs to be mindful of saying anything gossipy or negative, since the listener may be a second cousin of the person under discussion. Social awkwardness notwithstanding, there's nothing that beats sitting down with a cold beer in the dark Miners Bar for hearing stories of people in Hartville, Sunrise, and surroundings. These nearly empty communities will never be ghost towns as long as people talk about them as though they are still thriving.

Hartville is near the top of a winding road through Eureka Canyon six miles north of the town of Guernsey, a place nearly swallowed up by a Wyoming National Guard training camp. Only a couple dozen residents remain in Hartville, a town that comprises a few houses, a town hall, a bar, and a scattering of historic buildings such as the Hartville Jail. Hartville is Wyoming's oldest continuously incorporated town, having been founded in the 1870s and incorporated in 1884. The Miner's Bar boasts that it is the oldest bar in Wyoming, which is really a way of saying the back bar is the oldest in the state, having been shipped over in pieces from Germany and reassembled in Fort Laramie in 1864, then later brought here. The building itself seems to have been formed from a rockslide down the cliff. It would appear that where the rocks landed in a heap, an opening was gored through the rubble and that's how the bar was constructed.

Bar owners Lacy and Scott have had the place since about 1997, and keep it open only during summer weekends. The rest of the time they live and work in Douglas, about fifty miles away in Converse County. That leaves plenty of time for them to dedicate to running the bar, the name of which they shortened from Miners and Stockmans Bar just to Miners Bar.

To unruffle the feathers of any stockmen who might feel slighted by the omission, they unboxed a stash of historic burnt-wood livestock brands and restored them prominently to their spot on the walls of the bar, where they once were hung. The brands had been removed by a previous owner who had a grudge against area stockmen.

According to Lacy, the previous owner had been so annoyed by the stockmen he'd threatened to burn all the brand signs. So his wife took them all down and stashed them in the bar's basement, where they were safe from his pyrotechnical urges.

Lacy explains that part of the reason they bought the bar was to preserve area history, from the wooden brand signs to the priceless back bar to other rare and storied antiques around the building. "We didn't just buy a business. We bought antiques."

But she and Scott do have a bar business, thanks to a loyal group of local customers and occasional curious tourists. She says she's glad not to be open too much, having to face a crowd of barflies who, at other sorts of places, land on a stool each morning and imbibe throughout the day. She sees her customers just enough now to be genuinely glad when they walk through the door.

No matter how many hours a week the bar is open, over the years hundreds of customers have had a chance to write their names on a dollar bill and affix it to the ceiling. The urge to memorialize oneself can be seen in modern day graffiti, done with spray paint and using a language decipherable only to knowing readers. Whether a symbol that looks like a red and purple runic letter that has sprouted a tail denotes anything or not, its connotation is clear. Someone came here and claimed this spot for himself, and by golly no one had better get in the way.

The belligerence of marking one's claim to someone else's property with spray paint is not what's at play in the bar, however. Here, one's name joins a brotherhood of others who've come to this place, enjoyed its hospitality, and undertaken an informal but permanent ritual to join the club. Leaving a dollar bill stuck to the ceiling signed with one's own name is a way of paying dues to that club and being a member for life.

Similarly, passersby on the Oregon Trail recorded their names at a spot called Register Cliff, just outside of Guernsey. They were celebrating their crossing of the North Platte River, having journeyed from homes in

Indiana, or Illinois, or other places east. They spent weeks or months walking or riding in a wagon, families and livestock and neighbors moving west together toward Oregon territory across the hot, humid prairies alive with nipping critters. No wonder when they got to this spot they stopped long enough to leave notes to fellow travelers bringing up the rear.

The area near Register Cliff where the river was wide and shallow was a well-known and eagerly anticipated spot where travelers could stop, rest, and scrub some long-overdue laundry. After they crossed that river they would have new challenges, namely mountain passes and native people who might not be so happy to see yet another wagon train headed their way. But those worries could wait long enough to scratch initials or names, and a date, into the soft chalky limestone of Register Cliff.

Historic preservationists have gone to lengths to discourage modern day travelers from scratching their own names and dates into this cliff, and other similar sites along the emigrant trail. For the most part they've succeeded. However, there are still plenty of people who can't resist the self-memorializing urge, and we can learn more than we want to know about the relationship of Jason and Jennifer, and the doings of the class of '85, by reading their markings. The dominant motive for such etchings still seems to be the urge to say, "Hello, how are you? I am fine," like on a vacation postcard from Hawaii. The walls and ceilings and dollar bills of the Miners Bar are just another spot for those sorts of messages and stories to be told across time.

Bar stories are also told by the usual method—customers speaking to one another in real time, on adjoining barstools. On the day of our visit to the Miners Bar, we had a good chance to visit with Lacy in that manner before other customers arrived. Soon, a group of local folks came in and took up residence at a table toward the back of the bar, between the pool table and the jukebox, two ever-present pieces of bar decor. We didn't get much chance to talk to these folks, but then the very next day we visited the Guernsey State Park, and were prowling through the massive stone and log Civilian Conservation Corps structure that shelters the park's museum. Sure enough I recognized two or three of the group from the day before at the Miners Bar, wandering the museum grounds with us. The very next day we stopped for dinner at a bar in Guernsey and were at the counter settling up, when I exchanged a glance with a man at the bar.

"You look familiar" I told him. "Yeah, I saw you the other day at Hartville!" And with that, he and a woman seated next to him burst into the most diabolical diaphragm-wracking laugh I'd heard since The Shadow knowingly bwa-ha-ha'd about how much evil lurked in the hearts of men. I'm still not sure if I was a punchline to some alcohol soaked joke or just another reason to laugh it up on a small town Saturday night.

We heard another story at the Miners Bar, this one about the Sunrise Mine that is just a mile up the road. Sunrise was once a going little town, home to a mine that operated from 1899 to 1984. The mine, and thus the town, was owned by the Colorado Fuel and Iron Corporation.

Emigrants from Italy, Greece, Ireland, Japan, Lebanon and England mined copper from the open pit mine. Later they also mined iron ore from an underground operation. At its peak, seven hundred workers worked three shifts, and could extract as much as two thousand tons of iron ore a day.

Sunrise had a store, a doctor, a school, and the first YMCA in the state, which locals still talk about with nostalgia and longing. Many of the descendants of those immigrants remain in the area but now the townsite has been closed off by its owner, Fred Ells of Boulder, Colorado. His intention in restricting access is to protect the site from vandalism. There is occasional talk that the mine could reopen, but meantime its story is more about sunset than sunrise.

We heard more about Sunrise from a man named Joe whom we found attending the ticket booth at Guernsey State Park. The reservoir off the North Platte River that forms the recreational centerpiece of the park is drained each July to supply water for irrigation, so Joe was rather lonely in his tiny white ticket booth on that boatless afternoon. When we pulled up, we distracted him from a gaudy-covered Western paperback novel, but he didn't seem to mind the intrusion.

We told Joe about the bar tour and were only mildly surprised to hear that not only did he once work at the Miners Bar, he was raised in Sunrise and used to work in the mine. His father and grandfather were miners there, too. When Joe was a boy he played basketball for the school team. Away games were the only occasions Joe ever had to leave town.

"If we went on the road to someplace like Ft. Laramie, we'd get to have a meal on the road. That was something," he recalled wistfully. He also remembered the moment he first realized how "out in the sticks" Sunrise was. He'd joined the military during the war, and was serving in South Carolina with people from very different backgrounds. "Some boys suggested going on a 'coon hunt.' I thought they meant raccoons, but then I figured out that's not what they meant. I thought they were crazy then and I still think they're crazy now." Joe was happy to return to Wyoming after that experience, where he felt a little more at home.

Joe has spent most of his life in the area where he was raised, and is happy to tell stories and hand out maps and brochures to anyone who visits the park. When he mentions the YMCA, he seems sentimental about those old days in a place that held so much fun for mining families but is now just so much crumbling brick and plywood. We drove off with a wave, and Joe went back to his Western, with its cowboy heroes, beady-eyed villains, trusty steeds, and pure womanhood there for the defending.

Times really haven't changed all that much for many residents of the West, at least in this part of it. That's one reason Lacy is so adamant about keeping the bar's history intact for the future. She says if they ever sell the bar, they'll have it in the contract that the antique back bar must remain in the building, not be sold to the highest bidder and removed.

When she says "I'm from here," which she said many times during our visit, she doesn't seem to mean simply that she was born in the area. She means her family is from here, her ancestors are from here, her descendants will be from here. They may leave and move to a larger town, or join the military and see some more of the world, but their history is here and their future is here, too. They embody the expression that they'll "never meet a stranger" at the bar, the museum, or the donut shop in Guernsey. Compared to the college-town transience of my home of Laramie, Hartville has all the historic dust about it of a medieval English castle. That dust blends in with the dust of the sage plains and the mines and forms a mortar that binds the people to the soft limestone under their feet.

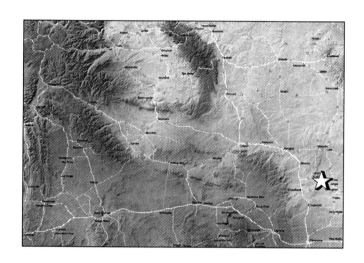

Ghosts
The Tavern
Ft. Laramie, Wyoming

Ron and I walked through the front door of the Tavern in Ft. Laramie, into an empty restaurant decorated in antique Western Victorian, complete with framed pictures of stone faced strangers and lace tablecloths. Entering the Taven from the back door at the same time was a man we'd just chatted with out in the street, and thought we'd said farewell to.

A big man dressed in even bigger overalls, he'd crossed the street to ask how we liked our small Toyota RAV4. If it was comfortable on road trips. If it got good gas mileage. If it could carry large-ish pieces of iron pipe and two-by-fours. If a man his size would be comfortable in it, or if he'd do better in a PT Cruiser.

"You look good in there," we told him, after we realized the polite thing to do was offer him a chance to get behind the wheel, and he obliged us. Our dog was settled on his blanket in the back seat. Otherwise our new friend might have left us there and taken the RAV4 and Spike out for a spin around the nineteenth century fort the town was named for.

Instead, he climbed back out of the car and we said our goodbyes. We took different paths into the Tavern: we the route through the front door, like customers; he the route to the back door, like a neighbor. When we met in the middle we smiled with surprise at meeting again so soon.

He led us down the dark staircase, past beer posters and a forty-gallon fish tank that softly bubbled and glowed, down the steps to the low-ceilinged basement and a bar with a padded vinyl front. Scattered tables and chairs around the room stood empty for now, but men there for an afternoon visit warmed a few of the barstools. They were drinking beer and talking, and another man leaned against the back bar wiping glasses with a white dishtowel. In a different place I'd identify these men as customers and bartender, but the Tavern is so much like anyone's basement at home that their relationship was less one of commerce than of neighborliness.

We soon blended into the conversation with bar owner Danny and his friends. I don't have much to contribute to stories about electrical work and other types of skilled labor, but Ron can sound like he knows what he's talking about on just about any subject. Eventually, talk turned to what he and I were up to, and we explained that we were on a bar tour of Wyoming. We mentioned our stop at the Miners Bar up the road in Hartville, where we'd been the day before.

"That's my daughter Lacy, who owns that place," Danny told us.

We hadn't expected to meet the father of the woman we'd found so pleasant at our previous bar tour stop, and we'd had no reason to wonder if she had a dad who ran a bar just a few miles away. We could see the resemblance, though. Both had waving brown hair and fine featured faces, with wide eyes like figures in a Byzantine mosaic. When Danny heard we'd met his daughter, he opened up with lots of family stories about his parents and grandparents who'd grown up in this country, about his kids, and about the neighbors in town who hang out in his basement. Before the afternoon was over we'd heard a lot of stories, and told lots of stories of our own. We'd become part of the Tavern family, settled into the basement rec room, if only for the day.

In my own family when I was a child, my parents' friends rarely came to visit. I wasn't aware of them having that many friends, which struck me as unthinkable coming from a clique-dominated childhood where a lack of friends meant social death. Looking back, I suppose that most of their friends were left behind in other cities as my father's sales job transferred him around the South and Midwest.

We had a basement in the house where I grew up, but there was no bar in it. There was a washing machine, but no dryer, because my mother was convinced nothing could beat air drying. Yards and yards of clothesline and several wooden drying racks filled most of the basement. Maybe a bar could have occupied some of that space instead of stiff clothes, except my parents didn't need one because they didn't drink. I recall my parents sipping a glass of wine for special occasions, such as the marriages of my older siblings, but never more than one glass. A can of Schlitz malt liquor sat for years in the back of my family's refrigerator, until rust corroded the can top. I don't know where it came from, or the circumstances when it finally went away.

Looking back I'm glad my parents were wholesome, sober, and there to keep an undistracted eye on me every night of the week and weekends, too. But there seemed to me then something a little dull about parents who were so steady, so predictable. My father got home from work at 5:15 every weekday evening, and within a half-hour of his arrival my mother would be placing on the table the filling but bland meal she'd spent her day trying to be inspired to prepare. My mother had once been a creative and willing cook, but after four children and too few special meals in restaurants, she'd run out of ideas. Her inspiration dwindled and her various intestinal illnesses eliminated spicy ingredients from her culinary arsenal, so by the time I came up, we were in a rotation of meatloaf, various casseroles topped with Chun King noodles, and vegetables that came out of cans.

After dinner my mother, sister and I tidied the kitchen then went to our own routines to try to fill the remaining very long evening. My sister got a job and a car to get her there as soon as she was old enough, so most evenings she was not at home. My mother sat at the kitchen table playing solitaire while listening to Royals baseball on the radio or watching the little television she kept there. My father shuffled through office paperwork, sitting at a card table set up in the living room. Eventually he'd transfer to a comfortable easy chair and, most evenings, doze off in front of the huge Mediterranean console television set. I'd go to my room and listen to Judy Garland records while doing homework, or hole up in the basement surrounded by my father's dress shirts, heaped in a pile for me to iron for twenty-five cents a shirt. That's how the family spent its evenings. Bedtime, when it came, was a mercy.

Some evenings after dinner I would visit Suzy, who lived just across the street of our zoysia-lawned suburb. We were the same age but went to different schools. I attended St. Agnes a few blocks away until ninth grade when I was enrolled in the Catholic high school that loomed even closer to my home than the grade school. Suzy was of some vague Protestant denomination, vague to me, anyway, and she attended the public grade school, but only through sixth grade. Then she went to junior high, a level of academic sophistication for which there was no equivalent in my parochial school, with its first through eighth grade students all lumped into the same building.

Everything about Suzy was sophisticated, compared to me. She was tall and tan with long brunette hair; I was short and skinny and the color of oatmeal. She had an exotic beauty, like Ali McGraw in *Love Story*. She was a cheerleader, and in fifth grade had been given the first of a series of ID bracelets, each signifying a new steady boyfriend. Suzy had a good looking older brother, and even though he only ever greeted me with a grunt when I rang their front doorbell, I still blushed to talk to him.

Suzy's father was a dentist, wore a gold man-bracelet, and always smelled like soap. Her mother was a beauty. She'd been an airline stewardess before she finally settled down at age twenty-nine to marry Suzy's father.

Everyone at that time knew that the job of airline stewardess was reserved for only the most beautiful, most poised, most elegant women. Only marriage to a handsome, successful man would have been a thinkable alternative, and Suzy's father was such a man.

Suzy's parents frequently went out on Saturday nights to parties at their friends' houses, leaving Suzy and her brother alone for the evening with a reminder to brush their teeth. Suzy's parents drank socially, but not excessively. Suzy's parents had parties of their own sometimes. Suzy's parents had a Bar in their Basement.

I like to imagine the crowd at the Tavern that afternoon we spent in Ft. Laramie as guests at one of Suzy's parents' parties. Like characters in a John Cheever story about the sophisticated and inscrutable life of suburban society, they'd swim through the evening, fish in a tank. Tetras, guppies, goldfish: all would glide and turn together trying to place one another's species in the social ecosystem.

Suzy's dad would be behind the bar most of the time, but he'd like to get out and mingle. In my imagination, I can see Danny spelling him for awhile, opening beers, uncorking wines, and mixing Manhattans and gimlets for the guests.

Suzy's dad had a Playboy themed bar, including a large mirror with the Playboy bunny trademark logo. He had glassware that depicted a beautiful Playboy bunny on the front, and on the back of the glass, a keyhole was etched into the frosted surface. As liquid from the glass was consumed, the Playboy bunny was revealed in a different, more titillating pose. Into those glasses I can imagine Danny pouring tall cold cocktails for the guests, who would drink with the goal of seeing what they could reveal.

Once or twice, Suzy and I were asked to help out and serve hors d'oeuvres to the guests when her parents had parties. We'd walk around with platters of cheese spritzed from a can onto little crackers, or cocktail wieners impaled with cellophane-tailed toothpicks. Women's long full skirts, pink and orange and green with floral patterns like flowerbeds overdosed with Miracle-Gro, would block our view of who was beckoning us for which delicacy.

Suzy's parents invited lots of people to their parties I didn't know. A few of them were from the block. I think my parents might have been invited as a polite gesture to their daughter's friend's parents, but I know they never attended. Looking back, I suppose most of the guests were professional associates of Suzy's father. They were around the same age as Suzy's parents and wore suits or long dresses to the parties. They drank and smoked and laughed, and said things to Suzy and me that we didn't understand as we passed the trays.

Albert, from the Tavern, would have been a big help at those affairs at Suzy's house. Albert is a resident of Ft. Laramie who holds so many jobs it seems the town would need to call in FEMA if he ever moved away. Albert is in his early thirties and handsome in a devilish sort of way, and could be even more so if he'd had Suzy's dad as a dentist. Uneven or missing teeth mar his smile a bit, but even so, his energy and many talents make him a good guy to have around. In Fort Laramie, he works at the town's only gas station each day, in the morning. Then in the afternoons he comes into the Tavern to help Danny.

The Tavern's restaurant prides itself on serving fine steak dinners, and Albert is the cook. He finishes that work just in time for his night job. He "rides ditches" from eleven p.m. to four a.m., which means he drives up and down the roads that run along the irrigation canals that take water from the Platte River into Nebraska. His job is to look for leaks that might prevent some of Wyoming's water from going to its legal owner to the east. In between times, Albert works on his electronics repair business, which he does on a freelance basis. That was his real job when he lived in Lake Tahoe, before he "lost" his wife and moved to Ft. Laramie, nearer his folks. If he'd been part of my childhood, Albert could have come to Suzy's parents' party. He would charm Suzy's mother, helping her warm the sweet and sour meatballs, adjusting the knobs on the basement hi-fi to get Herb Alpert and the Tijuana Brass set to the brightest levels.

Danny would have been a popular bartender at Suzy's parents' party. He'd tell men and women lined up at the bar astonishing stories over their martinis and Tom Collinses. About how he was born in a tin hut on a ranch at Lance Creek, Wyoming, just a dot on the map. "Don't let the dot fool you—there's really not much there." The doctor got there too late to attend the delivery, so Danny's mother did the work of birth with the help of Aunt Opal. Not long after, that doctor killed himself. Danny isn't sure whether or not he was to blame for the suicide, but the guests at Suzy's parent's party would have loved the story and asked Danny to mix another round. As he did so, he would tell them another story about his grandmother. About how when she was still a young woman, she was tragically killed. She'd been outside at the ranch checking on livestock in a storm, when a bolt of lightning struck her dead.

Danny would open a Budweiser with a church key, and add "One of my brothers also died an accidental death a few years back. It was rough coming up, but that is how my family has always lived."

If Danny and Albert had been to a party at Suzy's house, they would have brought along a friend who is a disabled veteran. Danny would have mixed the friend Canadian Club cocktails every few minutes. The friend has gray hair that scraggles down his neck but has nearly vacated the top of his head. He has wide shoulders over a very thin chest, and resembles a piece of bread that had been left in a toaster too long.

He talks quite a bit, but doesn't mind much if no one listens to him. Most of his talk is about the lawn mowing jobs he has lined up for himself after the next drink, after the party is over, maybe tomorrow when it cools off some.

Someone would ask him how he became disabled. He'd tell his story to the party guests. "It was 1969, and it was just my third day in Vietnam. That night they sent me down the river on a patrol boat. I wasn't wearing my helmet. A sniper spotted me in the dark and shot me in the head. They'd warned me not to light that cigarette."

"That's why they call him Gunshot Bob," Albert would explain.

Everyone at the party would laugh and slap Albert on the back. Someone would ask to feel the ridge in Gunshot Bob's head where the bullet scraped the bone. Suzy's dad would fix Gunshot Bob another CC. One of his doctor associates would offer to take a look at that scar.

Eventually Suzy's parents' party ends, and the guests go their various ways. Suzy and I grow up. She marries a few times and has two daughters. I marry a few times and have no children. She moves across the country but returns to our home town, where she still lives. I move to Wyoming, where I stay. Her parents divorce about the time she starts college. My father dies about the time I start college, and my mother lives alone in the house where I grew up. Suzy's father remarries but divorces again. Her mother drinks a bit too much, Suzy sometimes worries. New people move in and out of Suzy's parents' house, and my mother never meets them.

Meanwhile, back to present party at the Tavern: Danny shows us photographs on the wall of his downstairs bar. He has photos of his parents, his siblings and his grandparents. They are arranged in rows and columns, like a visual family tree. Among some of the photos hang memorabilia from his military service. The photo of his wide-eyed mother bears a striking resemblance to his daughter Lacy.

After a beer we admit we are hungry, so Danny goes upstairs to the kitchen to fix us buffalo burgers, and while he's busy with that, Gunshot Bob takes over bartending duty and serves us two more cold beers. We all talk about the street dance scheduled for that evening in Ft. Laramie. It is supposed to be a good time, and Gunshot Bob explains that the cops "never really bother anybody as long as you don't bother them." After we finish our burgers it is time to say so long to the gang and head back up the stairs, past the fish tank and the hopeful antiques, back to the dog sleeping in the car parked on the shady street.

As we disappear up the steps toward the back door we hear Gunshot Bob say to Danny and Albert: "Now those are good people. I hope they come back."

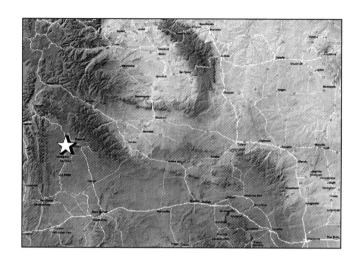

Cole Slaws All Around
Green River Bar
Daniel, Wyoming

The Green River Saloon in Daniel is more than just a bar. It is also a library, a bank, a movie theatre, and a great place to get any food item topped with slaw. It's a place to talk about the price of milk and eggs and voice opinions about whether Jeff Gordon or Richard Petty is the greatest NASCAR driver ever. It has a jukebox with entries ranging from Dean Martin to Tom Petty, and a pool table positioned mercifully in a side room away from the watchful eyes of folks who actually can finish a game in less than thirty minutes.

We learned all these things about the Green River Saloon in a late-May visit one weekday afternoon. After taking the scenic view up from Rock Springs via Big Piney (attempting to understand what makes that place

frequently shatter cold-temperature records, but failing)
we were spending a couple days at a Fremont Lake cabin
near Pinedale. After a two-hour hike around the Soda Lake
Wildlife Refuge, which teems with waterfowl and lake
critters, we were ready for a bar stop.

Some of the most scenic tourist attractions in an
area can go unexplored by locals. For example, Martha at
Leiterville had never been to Devil's Tower, not far east of
where she's lived a good chunk of her life. Ron and I avoid
Yellowstone National Park in summer because of the
crowds, and instead spend time in the national forests that
border the Park itself. Soda Lake is an undiscovered
though beautiful place, although on a smaller scale than
Yellowstone. None of the several folks in the bar at the time
knew anything about it. Maybe that explains why we were
alone during the duration of the hike. No matter. An
attraction almost as interesting could be found right here.

We arrived hungry and thirsty and sat at the bar,
facing into a back bar mirror and lots of bottles of exotic
liquors no one seems to order in Wyoming bars. I took the
advice of the bartender, who assured me that anything on
the menu topped with coleslaw couldn't be beat, so I
ordered the slaw dog.

I've always been adventurous with food combina-
tions, although I avoid anything that still has eyeballs or
was part of something's digestive system. Ron went with
the non-slaw burger even though according to everyone
there, "The slaw burger is even better than the slaw dog."
I declared to all who would listen that the slaw dog was the
best thing I'd ever eaten, and I wasn't lying—cool creamy

all-cabbage slaw helps anything glide down the throat, like a digestive waterslide.

As we munched and sipped beers we listened in on the conversations of the few other people who were in the bar for lunch or a cold brew. This from one weathered local ranching couple having lunch: "We love milk. Sometimes we drink a gallon a night with dinner, but these days you just can't afford it."

We eased ourselves into the conversation slowly, the way you enter a swimming pool when you don't know if it is heated or freezing. The others threw us a rope and pulled us in, perhaps as a result of our signal: "We're on a bar tour of Wyoming." Few other words cause people in bars to so quickly move over to your end of the bench, so to speak, and pat you on the back with stories about the history of their favorite place.

Turns out the Green River Bar has been around since 1899. It has seen generations of families through winters when you'd need a secured rope to cling to on your way from house to barn during a blinding blizzard. It's been there through world wars and peace marches, through energy booms and busts. People would come in with paychecks to cash and spend, earned from jobs at ranches or the oil patch. Kids could come in and play games and eat, as long as they sat at the tables and not at the bar.

These days a karaoke night draws extra folks one night a week, but the locals in the bar on this day weren't sorry to hear that event was about to be discontinued. They recall fondly the days before the bar got cable television, when Monday night was Movie Night at the Green River Saloon. They'd rent Westerns or suspense movies, and the place would swarm with grown ups and their kids, eating snacks (presumably not popcorn topped with slaw) and watching gunfights and tumbleweeds on the screen. The night they showed *The Rounders* starring Glenn Ford and Henry Fonda, "the place was filled up."

On the day of our visit, to keep the movie tradition alive, Willie Nelson and Delta Burke were soundlessly keeping the West safe from ne'er-do-wells on the TV above the bar.

Another bar tradition is reading and borrowing books from the Joe Hausen Library. Joe was a local and an avid reader, who was given shelf space in the bar to house his overflow books. What started as a few box loads has turned in to a library of at least a thousand volumes, shelved near the pool table. A wooden plaque with the name of the library burned into it stands across the top of one shelf. The library works on an honor system. We were invited to take what we wanted and return it next time we were passing through. No matter if it was a year from now. "Just come back sometime with the book and bring more for the collection, if you want."

People who don't spend much time in bars for reasons other than vigorous drinking might do a double take at the sight of somebody hanging out in a quiet corner with a cup of coffee and a Reader's Digest Condensed version of *Shane*. To me it made perfect sense. I've long used reading for cover when I'm alone somewhere in public. How many napkins, menus, sugar packets, or beer labels have I read, gazing into the middle distance between texts, wishing for a really good book.

For a time after graduate school I was a regular in a bar where I knew no one, but which offered great live blues and jazz on Saturday afternoons. A weekly event for me was to make a stop at the local library branch to check out a book, then carry it to Harling's Upstairs Bar & Grill to read in a corner while live music revved with the decibel force of a small airplane. How much more convenient it would have been for me if the books would have been available right there in the bar.

Instead of reading novels, I should have spent more time in those earlier bar going days practicing that beguiling game of pool. Ball, stick, hole: how hard could it be? A must-do at each stop on the bar tour is a game of pool, so we dutifully went into the pool room/library only to find a man there emptying both the table and the juke of money for counting and collecting. We thought we'd be turned away, but he magnanimously allowed us to play both the jukebox and a free game of pool. While I fired up Dean Martin tunes and Ron took several unsuccessful stabs at his stripes, the money man sat chatting with us, all the while casually counting stacks of bills towering several inches high, and enough piles of coins to make the wealthy Croesus jealous.

The vending machine man's Cowboy Cadillac idled in the parking lot, waiting to take him to the next stop on his run to other coin machines in bars around the area, lightening each machine considerably. Maybe he thought our pathetic efforts to knock in the 8-ball half an hour after the initial break was really a diabolical plot on our part to distract him and get his attention away, just for a moment, from all that dough. But no, the truth is, we come by our poor pool playing honestly. His cash was safe.

None of our bar friends appeared to hold us in lower regard after our pool display, however, and they cheerfully suggested other Wyoming small town bars we should visit on our tour. They were happy to load us up with bar T-shirts and matchbooks, and graciously let us take a few photographs inside the bar. After a stop in the restrooms (signed Daniel Airport Waiting Room, even though there is no airport in this town of fewer than four hundred residents) we were on our way. Saying goodbye to this gang and driving off felt to me not much different than saying goodbye to my own family after a visit back home. The same regret for not being able to stop back in tomorrow; the same flip in the stomach wondering where I'm headed next. Or maybe it was just the cole slaw.

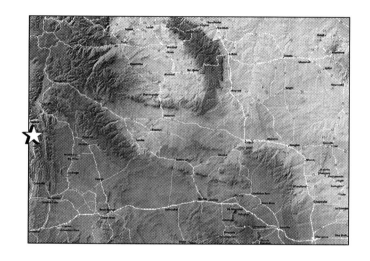

You Don't Have To Be Crazy, But It Helps
Dad's Bar
Thayne, Wyoming

Thayne is one of a dozen communities situated in western Wyoming's Star Valley, which it shares with the Star Valley Cheese Company, Olympic wrestler Rulon Gardner, and gun manufacturer Freedom Arms. White pioneers settled the Valley in the 19th century, in the form of Mormon missionaries from the Church of Jesus Christ of Latter-day Saints (LDS). The Mormons came into the Valley around 1880, and have had a pretty good grip on it ever since. They are widely known as serious and industrious workers, dedicated to home and hearth, and vigorously not in favor of liquor consumption.

Compared to their counterparts in Utah, Mormon communities in Wyoming are hippie compounds, with longhairs swinging in hammocks and smoking whatever comes in handy, metaphorically speaking. Mormons didn't settle Wyoming, but they settled Utah, and the Church's doctrine has had a powerful influence on its civic and social life ever since.

But as more non-Mormons move into the state, attracted by the natural beauty of mountains and canyons and the flourishing urban area of Salt Lake City, some bending of rules has taken place. One obvious adjustment involves alcohol consumption. When the 2002 Winter Olympics were held in Park City, Utah, area organizers practically panted their announcement to international sports fans: "Whoopie—you can have a glass of wine with dinner in Utah!" Tourists and the dollars they bring can be accommodated, even in the Beehive State.

Thayne and the other communities of Star Valley are peopled by lots of members of the LDS church. Star Valley was once just a mountain-framed bucolic area farmed by Mormon saints. It still is that, but now is under the influence of newcomers to affluent Jackson Hole or visitors to Yellowstone and Teton national parks. Locals, tourists, and wealthy part-time residents may be expected to tip a cocktail at sunset or sip a cold beer after whitewater rafting down the Snake River. Happily, a balance has been struck between the religious lifestyle of the Mormons and the other residents of, and visitors to, the Valley.

We'd come to Thayne after several days in Salt Lake City, where one needed the powers of a water buffalo with a divining rod to sniff out a restaurant or bar that served full-strength beer. We were in Salt Lake as presenters at a professional conference called *Shaping the American West*, and we were delighted to tell our audience of academics all about our bar tour of Wyoming, and show pictures of some of our favorite barscapes. Lots of "oohs" at the scenic shots of locales, lots of "aahs" at the rustic bars and their rusty decor. More than a little bit of envy that we'd thought up such a fun project and found a way to convince the academic community that it was "research." After several days attending that conference in crowded Salt Lake, with its hazy sky and manic drivers, we were glad to head back to Wyoming.

Many years ago I was on a road trip from Kansas into Colorado and on in to Wyoming. I planned to head into Wyoming on a Sunday morning and I wondered if, like Kansas, liquor stores in Wyoming were closed on Sundays. If so, I'd be buying beer in Colorado before crossing the state line. I asked a wide-eyed young waitress where I'd stopped for dinner in Colorado about Wyoming liquor laws. She told me: "In Wyoming you can do anything you want, anytime you want to do it." Boy, that's a set of rules that appealed to me, and seemed sublimely antithetical to the Midwest I was then planning to escape. Even now those words are Siren songs to me and I've come near to crashing against rocks trying to get back to my Wyoming home whenever I've had reason to leave its borders.

The waitress's assessment of Wyoming was in evidence at Dad's Bar in Thayne, the town we chose from the others in Star Valley because it also offered a couple motels and restaurants. Afton and Alpine have all that and more, but their abundance of bars took them out of contention as official stops on the bar tour. Uncomplicated Thayne has just two bars, The Pines, and Dad's Bar, which we chose above The Pines because it had been recommended to us at the Green River Bar in Daniel.

We showed up at Dad's on a rainy Sunday afternoon in June. We found seated at one end of the cool dark bar two men dressed in jeans, cowboy hats, and Western style silk neckerchiefs. The woman with them was similarly attired. At the opposite end of the bar sat two Latino ranch workers spiffily dressed in jeans and cowboy hats, sporting long mustaches. They were quietly speaking in Spanish to one another, but spoke in English occasionally when the woman tending bar suggested refills. We took up a position equidistant to those two groups, but fairly close to a friendly fellow named Mike.

Mike is a sturdy man in his mid-thirties with lots of dark hair—even more in his big beard than on his head. If you had a flat tire on the side of the road, he'd be the sort of guy you'd be glad to see pull up to help. Mike surely looks the part of a storybook Wyoming cowboy as he outfits dudes from California or Texas for horseback trips in the Tetons. That's summer; during winter he does general labor around the Valley.

Mike knows a lot about animals. In fact, he says veterinary work might have been his calling, had he attended college. He tells us that because of his inadequate finances and the passage of time, a college career is probably water over the dam. Mike consoles himself that his job as an outfitter gives him plenty of time to tend to animals, and he's almost as busy doing that during the outfitting season as any large animal vet.

Conversation is easy in most Wyoming bars, and we were happy to stop worrying about confounded Utah and instead to be chatting with Mike and company about grizzly bears, hunting, and fishing. We told our new friends about the bar tour and asked them what was the best thing about Dad's Bar.

The neckerchiefed men took turns declaring, "Me! I'm the best thing about Dad's!"

Mike chipped in with the town slogan: "We're not crazy—we're just in-Thayne!"

To see a history of Thayne, crazy or not, I just had to take a look around inside Dad's, which is something of a town museum. I poked around the bar that seemed to get larger the farther I wandered from the home base of my barstool. All around the walls of the place, framed photos featured racehorses and riders and spectators. Not Kentucky Derby style with silk colors and stringy thoroughbreds and ladies in funny flowered hats. These pictures showed cold weather racing, with blankets and breath in the air and horses drawing sleds mounted on long skis.

The photographs depicted a winter pastime known as cutter racing, said to have originated in Thayne in the 1920s. "Dad" didn't open his bar until 1933, but early on in cutter racing history the bar sponsored teams and hosted Calcuttas, which allowed patrons to bet on racers or horses. Cutter racing is a form of chariot racing like in the movie *Ben Hur*, but without the nasty daggers protruding from the hubs of enemy chariot wheels. In cutter racing, the driver rides in a small conveyance called a cutter or a sleigh. Some cutters glide on skis, others roll on wheels. The quarter horse team races down a quarter mile straightaway track through mud or snow. The competition is a great way to wile away short winter days during the long winter season, which can start in November and end in May.

A racing sleigh suspended over the front door outside the bar and silhouetted race teams painted on the outer wall testify to Dad's connection with the sport. However, there was talk in the bar that day about Dad's no longer sponsoring a cutter team, and even the end of cutter racing in Thayne. According to bar talk, there was too much bickering in the community for the folks at Dad's to feel confident the teams would be racing again come January. It would be a shame to end such a proud tradition, but like many rural pastimes, it may turn out to be a victim of either the waning volunteer corps or a change of tastes as new residents move in. But for now, divisiveness is a sadly common state of things.

Divisiveness is not uncommon in my own part of Wyoming, and my stories about the new non-smoking ordinance in Laramie got the regulars at Dad's so mad the bar rattled with the collective clatter of six hacking coughing smokers. In fall of 2004 voters in Laramie acted to make all public places in town non-smoking, including bars. That makes Laramie just like California and several communities in Colorado. That comparison is fightin' words to many Wyomingites, except to those the combatants might describe as "pointy-headed intellectuals and health nuts in Laramie, who might like it better in Boulder, Colorado with the other granola-eating tree huggers."

Some Laramie bar-owners and personal freedom advocates disagreed with the objectives of the granola eaters who pushed for the smoking ban, and after the election discovered what they hoped were voting irregularities. An election challenge failed, so the smoking ban went into effect in April 2005. I didn't vote for the ban. I don't smoke; I don't enjoy cigarette smoke. Nonetheless, I felt the legislation was too restrictive to business owners and that the argument that the law should be passed to protect the health of the downtrodden bartenders of Laramie was a smokescreen. And like many Wyomingites, I recoil a bit at being told what to do. The sad fact is, increasingly in Wyoming, one cannot do anything one wants to do, anytime one wants to do it.

The folks at Dad's, and at the other small bars around the state that are pretty much the whole town, wouldn't take too kindly to being handed a rule saying they couldn't have a smoke or two with their drinks. After all, those bars are their hangouts, their second homes. They are where news is exchanged and town activities are planned and local identity is formed. I have a very hard time picturing Mike and company shivering outside on the snowy sidewalk, huddled under the sheltering suspended cutter, puffing on cigarettes between drinks. They might as well stay home, smoking and drinking alone. Then where would the conversation be? Where would people go to visit friends and neighbors in a tiny town where most people live on far flung rural acreage? Very recently there's been talk about a statewide smoking ban in Wyoming. If this initiative picks up steam, and doesn't exempt bars, the bar tour might become a very lonely enterprise, and worse, the next cutter race will never be planned.

Meanwhile, smoking, drinking and conversation race on at Dad's in Thayne, taking in friends and newcomers. In this constellation of farming communities, newcomers stand out. More people are moving into the area, in fact, Alpine, just to the north, is Wyoming's fastest growing town, and the Valley itself is up to about seven thousand residents. But locals are still warmly tolerant of strangers.

As we were ready to leave Dad's, the bartender voluntarily got on the phone and called every restaurant in town to see who was open Sunday nights to serve us dinner. Everyone there said they hoped we'd come back after our meal, to continue our conversation with some more regulars who'd just come in as we were getting ready to leave.

When they entered, Mike leaned over and whispered to us, "Watch this. You can't leave yet—these folks are crazy."

The couple had been at the Pines Bar, evidentially for a few hours. They picked up on our conversation on the Laramie smoking ban. That led them into a hilarious (to us) argument over which was worse for the lungs: cigarette smoke or airborne cat hair.

We didn't make it back to the bar after dinner so I didn't learn the outcome of that particular debate. But somewhere along the line, someone must have decided whether they were willing to breathe cigarette smoke in the house, or put up with their partner's shedding cats. Someone had to make a rule, lay down a line, and compromise a position. Someone had to adhere to a system of belief, and put down a predictable series of "shalls" and "shalt nots." In that way, people can proceed through their daily life without constantly wondering if they are stepping over a moral or legal line, the way a basketball player with too big feet sometimes steps on the endline of the court and goes out of bounds.

My Colorado waitress must have been making a comparison to her own state when she said that Wyomingites can do anything they want, any time they want. Compared to her people-filled state, Wyoming must seem a land where rule books are mythical, like unicorns. Maybe the Mormons had the right idea when they hand-built their state using the clay of their religious beliefs. Everyone there knows what the rules are—there are no doubts. But maybe their regulations are a bit too stringent. After all, sometimes the difference between right and wrong isn't that hard to see.

The Bartender
Union Bar
Hudson, Wyoming

In a television commercial for a prescription sleep aid, a groggy man sits at his kitchen table and chats with Abraham Lincoln, a talking beaver, and an astronaut in full space-walk gear. Regulars from his dreams, they miss his visits to their land of sand while instead he lies awake, tossing and turning from insomnia.

Those disparate characters would fit right in among the crowd at the Union Bar in Hudson. Democrats in a mostly Republican state pondering the latest war news from the Middle East. Native Americans from the Wind River Reservation, whose border is about fifty yards north of the bar, spending a companionable evening with non-Indians from Hudson and from the nearby larger towns of Lander and Riverton. Folks from California who've sold their homes and with the surplus cash purchased property here in the foothills of the evocatively named Wind River Mountains. Folks who pan for gold in a stream right outside the back door of their weekend mountain cabin. Blue-collar workers who gather in the large back meeting room to talk business under the steady stares of famous political figures, captured in photographs. A fifth-generation Wyomingite who comes to the Union almost every evening regardless of weather. Another regular who tells complete strangers a story about how his leg got chewed up by a motorboat propeller, back in the 1960s. Generous customers who win the Shake-a-Day contest and buy everyone in the bar a drink with their $150 windfall. Bar tourists who can't seem to get enough of this place and make multiple trips just to soak up the atmosphere.

All of these folks appear on any given evening to chat with bar owner Mike Vinich. A Marine in World War II, Purple Heart recipient, and friend of the late President John F. Kennedy, Mike is Wyoming's most popular living bartender. Mike is the sort of bartender that everyone hopes knows them by their first name. He holds court at the only stand-alone bar in Hudson, home to four hundred people, one art gallery, a crazy-good steak house, and a post office.

Hudson sits on Wyoming Highway 789 about fifteen miles northeast of Lander and twenty-five miles southwest of Riverton. From the outside, the Union looks like a typical working-class Wyoming bar. The façade, painted a shade of beige that has no name, is broken by a few small windows mostly constructed of glass block, and a simple white wooden door. The Union Bar has been in the Vinich family for about forty years, and for longer than that, the family had the store that now stands unused in the brick building next door.

Mike's parents, John and Helen, met when John was serving in World War I. Helen was from Yugoslavia, and they married in Dubrovnic in 1919. After their marriage they came to the Hudson area. John worked in local coal mines which were once the backbone of this region. They eventually settled in Hudson and had five children, among them Mike.

We've been to the Union bar several times. The first time was on the recommendation of Phil Roberts. Phil is a Wyoming native and a history professor at the University of Wyoming. Along with his brother Dave, Phil is the author of *Wyoming Almanac*, which contains nearly every known fact about this state. When we told Phil about our bar tour project, he told us about a lot of wonderful out of the way bars in Wyoming. Phil doesn't get out as much as he used to, apparently. Our quests to some of them were wild goose chases to places long shuttered, perhaps leading to our next book: *Ghost Bars of Wyoming*. But we took Phil at his word that there was no place in Wyoming like the Union, a place with a blend of dissimilar and exotic customers second only to the cocktail lounge in the first *Star Wars* film.

The bar was as bustling as that famous cinematic scene on our first visit. We elbowed our way up to the bar for drinks then talked with people over the tunes coming from the always-free jukebox. We behaved like tourists, wandering the bar's long narrow main room and large square back meeting room, gawking at the photographs hung from floor to ceiling and squeezed in between mounted animal heads. Photos of the young Vinich family over the decades, photos of area mines, ranches, winter storms, wildlife, memorable moments at the Union, and of course, those politicians. Mike with JFK. Mike with notable Wyoming governors and other leaders of both party affiliations. Mike with his son, John, Union bartender and respected state legislator, dead too soon of a heart attack in 2004 at age fifty-three. John was one of the few non-agriculturists in the Wyoming legislature, where he was an advocate for the needs of people on the Reservation, and for the working class family in general. John is Wyoming's most popular bartender no longer living.

We never met the legendary John Vinich. Unfortunately, we didn't follow Phil Robert's suggestion to visit the Union Bar soon enough. It was August 2005 before we finally made the trip to Hudson.

Seated at the bar during that visit, we noticed a strange apparatus near the floor where a foot rail would normally be. The fifth-generation Wyomingite customer told us it was a urinal trough, a relic from the days when men found creative ways to keep ladies out of saloons. I knew these troughs once existed in bars back East because I saw them mentioned in a book I read while researching the subject of saloons. We wanted to ask Bobbi Jo, the other bartender, if she'd run the water through it for us, but we felt too touristy as it was.

Instead, we chatted with the fellow next to us. The one who'd been hurt in the motor boat accident.

He told me his story about cooling off in a local lake on a warm summer day. "There was one motor boat in the whole lake and I got hit by it." He had to be taken to a hospital in Casper, about 140 miles away. One outcome of the accident was that it made him category 4F for the draft. He didn't have to serve in the military or go to Vietnam. The guy who was driving the boat was a friend of his and wound up being wounded in the war. He later committed suicide.

People tell all sorts of stories like this one in bars. Some of them are deeply personal and most of them are unsolicited. I'm not repeating all the details of the story this man told me that night. Some of them are gruesome, and some of them may be painful to friends of the people mentioned. But a story is a story, and in bars a good story is more precious than currency.

Mike tells great stories, and he was telling them to someone else the evening of our first visit to the Union. We aren't the only ones who traveled from far away to hear Mike extemporize about subjects ranging from battles he was part of against the Japanese, to the state of modern politics. But on this first visit we weren't able to get close enough to join the listeners. After we had a few drinks, including one bought for us by the lucky winner of the Shake-a-Day, we headed two doors down to Svilar's, a restaurant that can best be described in terms of steak sizes and belt notches. We enjoyed the cabbage rolls and ravioli appetizers, emblems of the restaurant's Yugoslavian and Hungarian heritage, and the real bleu cheese dressing on our salads. We waddled out, too full to stop back by the bar to try our luck again with Mike.

We spent that night at a motel in Lander because there is no lodging in Hudson. We had wanted to take pictures that evening but it seemed awkward to start shooting photographs with no warning in that crowded bar. We took a chance that we'd be able to stop back in at the Union during the following day and see Mike.

When we got there around noon the bar was closed so we killed time shopping in Hudson's cornucopic art gallery, where we bought a nice bleached bison skull to hang on the wall of our guest room at home. As we were loading the skull into the car in a way that it wouldn't slide off the seat and gore Spike, Mike pulled up in a 1970s era land yacht and parked in front of the bar. We introduced ourselves and asked if we could come in just long enough to take a few pictures. He graciously obliged us and led us on our own private tour of the Union Bar.

Mike took us around both main rooms and stopped at key photographs hanging on the wall. Each photograph told a literal story. But each photograph had a back story that only Mike could tell. One photo showed a small group of boys in baseball uniforms, who turned out to be the first baseball team in Hudson, a cute group of kids, and one of the cutest unmistakably a very young Mike. Charming but not unusual, until Mike titillated us with the backstory. Turns out the coach used to work for notorious gangster Al Capone.

At another stop, Mike posed for a photo near an aircraft with a smiling John F. Kennedy, his hair tousled in the wind. "John Kennedy saved my life," was Mike's matter-of-fact explanation for that association. He paused here to tell us the details of his military service.

Mike served in the Pacific theatre during the war as part of the 1st Marine Paratroopers. In August 1942, when Mike was only eighteen, his unit landed on Guadalcanal to battle the Japanese for that piece of rock in the Solomon Islands. After the victory, his unit was part of another invasion on the islands of Vella Lavella and Choiseul.

This time, with heavy fire, the Japanese drove them out onto the beaches, where they signaled for help from the U.S. Navy. A torpedo boat came to their rescue, none other than the famous PT-109, commanded by John F. Kennedy.

Mike told us his unit was next called to help in the invasion of Bougainville, led by Admiral William Halsey, which was instrumental in securing that area from the Japanese. Eventually Mike's unit went to Hawaii for more training, and from there, on to Iwo Jima. Mike was in the first wave of invaders and was seriously wounded by machine gun fire on his first day of battle on February 19, 1945. He was decorated with five battle stars, a good conduct medal, and the Purple Heart for wounds he received at Iwo Jima.

Mike's connection to President Kennedy continued when he was part of the fifteen-member Wyoming delegation that put Kennedy's nomination over the top during the 1960 Democratic convention. Mike later worked in the U.S. Capitol Building during the Kennedy administration.

On our most recent visit to the Union, at least one new photograph was hanging behind the bar. It was the photo Ron took of Mike the morning of our private tour. Ron framed the picture and mailed it to Mike with a note. Now the image hangs in the same spot where Mike was standing when the photo was shot, creating a picture within a picture kaleidoscope as it shimmers and reflects against the Tiffany back bar. When we saw it hanging there, we happened to be chatting with the folks who pan gold in the river right outside their mountain cabin. It was a handy icebreaker to disclose that Ron had taken that picture and that we were on a bar tour of Wyoming. We became quite chummy during our chat with the couple, but for some reason they never did give us that map to the cabin and its hidden reserve of gold.

Nearly every night, Mike holds court at the bar dressed in a zippered jumpsuit and a Purple Heart ball cap, allowing customers to buy him glasses of burgundy wine for his "health." On our last visit Mike wasn't there when we first arrived, but we had a great time getting to know more of the local folks and the ever-purring Vinny the cat, who took the stool next to me for awhile.

Eventually we went down the street to again eat too much steak, then returned to the sight of Mike sitting on a barstool with a couple empty stools right there, as though fate had just ushered a few other customers out the door to make room for us. With hugs and handshakes, Mike made us relative strangers feel right at home, and even bought us an after-dinner cocktail. As we sat together at the bar, he showed us a book that had been written about World War II battles in the Pacific theater. Mike's name was mentioned several times by the author. We felt awed by his heroism and proud to be part of Mike's extended bar family.

Mike was born on Leap Day and so puts his age at "twenty-something." In many ways that way of estimating Mike's age is more accurate than counting traditional years.

If my own father were still alive, he'd be just a few years older than Mike. Called "Bud" by friends and family, my father wasn't in the military as were most men his age. A heart murmur kept him on the ground, patriotically watching for enemy planes through binoculars trained at the unsullied Midwestern sky. That heart murmur eventually caught up with him, and he was dead at sixty from complications of cardio-vascular disease.

My father, like Mike, was a great storyteller. A salesman of the old school, Bud traveled a large Midwestern region taking orders for small appliances to be sold by retailers. Once a year he'd take the family on a car vacation. He struck up jolly conversations in countless Holiday Inn lobbies across America, confabbing with other men similarly kept waiting by wives and vacation-addled children.

Bud was a non-drinking Republican, but he would have loved the Union Bar. He could have sat and talked to Mike all night long. He respected any honest man who could inspire the kind of admiration Mike evokes all around him. Maybe that's because my father was the same way.

As I hugged Mike goodnight after our last visit to the Union, I gave a little extra squeeze. That hug's for you, Bud. You would have been a great bartender.

An Eye Opener
Eden Saloon
Eden, Wyoming

At the Eden Saloon in Eden, a town of 338 that's miraculously green amidst miles of sage covered prairie, a souvenir mug for sale in the bar offers a millenniums-old promise: *Warning: Contents of this mug will open your eyes to sights you've never seen.* The meaning of that promise is open to as many interpretations as one has imagination to spin out. For starters, once I see these new sights, will I ever be the same?

Maybe I had too much time to contemplate when we visited the Eden Saloon on a cool May weekday afternoon. The lushness of the towering cottonwood trees, the only living thing standing taller than an antelope within miles of this spot, got me thinking of that famous garden named Eden. It was there that another warning about the dangers of imbibing was sounded. When God told Adam and Eve not to eat apples growing on the tree of knowledge, was he telling them doing so would open their eyes to sights they'd never seen? Was he saying they'd be better off not knowing about morbidity and mortality and other things in store for humanity? Of course, the snake selling curiosity got the better of them, and his appeals to Adam and Eve's need to know won out over blissful obedience. The snake played bartender in that ancient tale, with Adam and Eve as the first customers at his table. I can almost hear his slithery-tongued voice hissing: "This stuff'll make a man out of you. Don't say I didn't warn you!"

The name Eden makes it hard not to think in biblical terms, and ponder what tempted the Mennonite settlers who created this town back in the nineteenth century. They had good raw materials to work with on this dusty desert plateau, thanks to the streams of the Big Sandy drainage (with enough water to fill the Eden Reservoir they built). They'd just crossed an opening in the Wind River Mountains called South Pass (finally—a reasonable way to get over the mountainous barrier to travel West) and landed in an area of arresting natural beauty and plenty of possibility for making a living—for those who really worked at it.

The potential of the place today is the sort real estate agents refer to as of the "fixer upper" variety. There isn't much infrastructure in the area for developing large-scale human habitation, which is just as well. But archeologists believe the area has been home to humans for as long as six thousand years, citing evidence of bison-kill sites and petroglyphs on rock outcroppings in the area. In the nineteenth and early twentieth centuries the area stayed busy with travelers along the Oregon and Mormon trails and even with a brief flurry of Pony Express riders.

Irrigation that started in 1907 made ranching the success it is in the area even now. The Eden Reservoir has been improved and has been joined by several other larger reservoirs on other dammed rivers. Not damned in the biblical sense, of course, as far as we can tell so far. Today all that can be seen of the town of Eden from U.S. Highway 191 are a few houses and a smattering of other dusty structures. Dominant among those is the Eden Saloon.

We'd driven past this peeling painted place (let's be generous and call it blue) many times, in various seasons of Wyoming's always assertive climate. In winter the snow wafts across the roadway in snaking ribbons of white, making the center stripes dance a conga line on the concrete. In summer the desert surrounding Eden always is hot, even though the town is at an elevation of more than 6,500 feet. The boxcar-shaped Eden Saloon shimmers like a desert oasis in the heat waves that rise off the highway, but in this mirage tall shady cottonwoods replace spindly palm trees. A banner outside welcoming fishermen and advertising both kinds of beer (Budweiser and Coors) is hard to resist in any kind of weather, and yet many leisure travelers are capable of just that kind of self-control. Because like attracts, most tourists won't stop at a place without other recreational vehicles or mini-vans in Mastercard-fueled plenty. But local folks, occasional bands of bikers, and nuts like us on bar tours of Wyoming can always find a friendly barstool in Eden. And doing so often opens our eyes to sights we've never seen before.

For starters, just like Eden in the Bible, the Saloon is full of creatures of every description: furry ones, scaled ones, some with funny horns, some with noble stares. Unlike in that other Eden, though, none of these abundant creatures is able to walk or swim anymore, due to a lack of legs, limbs or tails long since removed by hunters, time or fate.

The Saloon was going through a facelift when we visited, in the form of interior paint, and the mounted critters had been taken from the walls and heaped without regard to predator-prey relationships and covered with plastic drop-cloths. At the time of our visit they were all in a decidedly undignified state, like a bunch of sorority sisters surprised in mud packs and bunny slippers by unexpected company. No matter—we were still given the grand tour and permission to photograph some of the more camera pleasing specimens.

We heard a story about one of the taxidermied creatures we photographed there—an orphaned bobcat named Doober. He'd been the pet of someone in town who'd bottle fed him since he was a week old, the story goes. Doober was a regular in the Saloon—he used to play on the pool tables and generally make himself at home. Doober spent some of his time leashed to a clothesline that allowed him to be out in the sunshine and also get a little exercise. Tragically, as sometimes happens to dogs rigged in this way, Doober got tangled up and hanged himself on the clothesline. The gang at the Saloon had been so fond of him, and was so saddened by his passing, that they decided he should be stuffed and kept forever in the bar. That's where he remains today, squinting through the smoky air at the Eden Saloon. It might not be heaven, but for Doober, keeping a watchful gaze on the people who loved him, it must at least beat the alternative.

Bars can be a haven, a home, a resting place. Yet I often meet people who never enter their doors for fear of being unwelcome, I suppose. For example, there is a bar in my town of Laramie that is something of a landmark. By night it fills with college students and locals and, truth be told, sometimes fights break out. There is a hole in the mirror behind the bar, punctured in the 1970s by a flying bullet and never repaired. The bar is on the National Register of Historic Places—not because of the bullet hole, but because it is in one of Laramie's oldest buildings. So that designation gives it a certain respectability, a certain panache. Yet I know so many people who have lived in Laramie for years, but never ventured in. I have become a tour guide to the underworld that is that bar for probably a dozen people during the last year. Recently I took such a group of friends in to the bar for the first time, in the safety of the daylight hours. I told them, "Don't act like tourists, and don't pick fights with the natives."

That's the only advice they needed, and they quickly fit right in among the stuffed bobcats, two-headed calves, and a bar regular who made a showily polite gesture of helping us ladies into our chairs. Before my friends knew it, they were lost in nostalgia, looking at the crossbar from the goal post that was carried to the bar on the night of a particularly rare victory of the UW football Cowboys over a particularly despised foe. If my friends stood on a barstool, they could read the signatures of all their friends and neighbors who joined that parade and wrote their names on the crossbar before it was hoisted up to hang parallel over the bar. The neophytes I introduced to this Laramie bar that day left glad they came, but somewhat wistful that the place turned out to be so...ordinary.

If we slow down and look, all of us could see sights we never expected to see. We don't have to absorb the contents of a souvenir mug, or migrate over mountain passes toward a promised land, to find revelation. Living life on one side of a fence can feel safe and familiar, but it is the other side that can be an eye opener. For example, maybe Eve could have stayed in the garden had she not bitten that fruit, but when life hands you apples, make apple pie. Maybe Mennonite farmers could have stayed in the flat lands, but had they not struck out across the prairie for parts unknown they never would have discovered the Eden Valley. Perhaps Doober the bobcat could have remained uncurious about what lay over the next ridge, then wouldn't have spun out his life on the end of a clothesline and crossed the Rainbow Bridge to his bobcat parents in animal heaven. Maybe a football team with a losing season wouldn't have found a way to defeat their arch opponent and watch their fans haul a symbol of their victory to the town's oldest temple. Maybe professors in a small college town would spend their beer dollars where the working folks hang out, instead of in the familiar safety of a local micro-brew. The grass on the other side is sometimes greener, but that green might just be crabgrass or fresh dollar bills growing from the soil. One can't tell from a cautious distance.

It is so easy to speed past the Eden Saloons of the world, not stopping because there are too few other vehicles in front, or because the vehicles that are resting there are Harley Davidsons rather than Honda Odysseys. Truth be told, lurking inside the Eden Saloon each afternoon are a very ordinary pair of mild-mannered women watching *The Young and the Restless* on television, and a white-haired lady named Josie who wiles away the hours at the end of the bar over a newspaper. Rather like what goes on inside many people's secure homes, each day.

I've been known to be too cautious, too, and have been guilty of "flying past" myself, always on the way to someplace that I've targeted, planned for, estimated, measured or reserved a non-smoking king-bedded room. Although those other places have been rewarding, there's always regret for the detour not taken, for not seeing whether the grass really is greener in the other valley. In this Eden paradise, succumbing to temptation puts you nose to nose with the unexpected, and looking straight into the face of a surprise.

The Messengers
Cactus Tree Pub
Granger, Wyoming

A Wyoming Bar Journey

The owners of the Cactus Tree Pub in Granger are people we should have known, but somehow didn't until we stopped at the bar in summer 2005. Ed and Jessica bought the only bar in town that spring. Before that they lived in Casper, but before *that*, until 1996, Jessica worked in our community of Laramie and lived in Centennial, about thirty miles west. Now, they run the little bar that serves a menu of pub food and caters to locals, energy workers, and itinerant ranch help.

The Cactus Tree Pub offers a cool, tidy haven far from the efficient but maddening I-80 with its semi-trucks and summertime behemoth travel trailers. A wizened cactus that stands near the pub's front porch evokes Jimmy Buffet music and clay coyotes in bandanas, with muzzles pointed straight up at the moon. Few travelers fall off the interstate and come the five miles north to Granger for services. Instead they motor on to Green River or Rock Springs to the east, or Evanston to the west. Too bad—this place beats generica along the highway any day of the week.

Both Ed and Jessica have a busy life outside owning and operating a bar. Ed has a full time job with an energy company out of Green River. That's why they live in nearby Granger, instead of somewhere a little less dry and weathered. The company he works for is the largest employer in this part of the state, occupying itself by mining a rock called trona, which eventually becomes soda ash, which eventually may become glass, or laundry soap, or any of dozens of other useful products. Ed's work schedule gives him eight days off in a row, which allows him to be a good hand at the Cactus Tree Pub.

Jessica is at the bar fulltime, and her side business involves making and selling scented and decorative candles to various retailers around the state. In the bar she has a glass-fronted case for the candles, the sort of cabinet that homemakers use to display stemware and china reserved for when company calls. The day we showed up at the Cactus Tree, we felt very much like company who'd stopped in unexpectedly but still were offered fresh apple pie and a sincere smile.

We arrived in Granger on an early afternoon in June. We were disappointed that a bar our friend Phil had told us about down U.S. 30 in Opal (pronounced O'Pal), appeared to have been boarded up for about twenty years. Faced with the future of heading back to I-80 and a landscape of mining operations and power plants, we stayed north of the main highway and proceeded east to a town small enough to harbor one good bar. If nothing else, the Wyoming highway map showed an 1860 Pony Express station and historical marker where we could have a car picnic out of the ever-blowing wind.

The Pony Express never would have lasted even its eighteen months if riders carrying mail had been as wimpy as we when it came to gusty wind and desert heat. We were glad they'd found this naturally sheltered layover on the mail trail from St. Joseph, Missouri to Sacramento, California.

Thanking the spirits of intrepid nineteenth century nation-builders, we munched raw vegetables, salty crackers, and chewy slices from a wheel of provolone bought at the Star Valley Cheese Company in Thayne. We fed Spike his favorite food, baby carrots, as he panted and wagged from the back seat. After we finished eating and brushed the cracker crumbs from the map, we noticed we were also very near the site of the 1834 Mountain Man Rendezvous. Their spot along the Blacks Fork River had some of the gentlest and most inviting terrain in Sweetwater County. That rugged mountain men would have bugged out from hunting camps and beaver traps long enough to get together for a big party not far from where we sat came as no surprise.

So, although we were almost deliriously happy to round the corner from the Pony Express Station and find the Cactus Tree Pub, we weren't surprised that such an oasis would exist here in this town of about 150 people. We went in prepared to toast the ghosts of Westerners past.

We got there about the same time Ed and Jessica were unloading their SUV, just back from a grocery supply run to Evanston, more than fifty miles west on I-80. I felt like I should have helped stow bags of potato chips and cases of beer, but I didn't know where anything went. And of course, I wasn't a family member and this wasn't my house or my bar. It just felt like it. Instead, we ordered a round of beers, and told Ed and Jessica about the bar tour. That led us to mention our Laramie home, and to open up the conversation to Jessica's time in Centennial, and their plans to retire there one day.

We talked about the glacial Medicine Bow Peak and the beauty of the surrounding alpine lakes. Land prices for home sites were held up to the light and examined in comparison to those in the Platte Valley and other scenic areas of Wyoming, with nothing about the subject matter left unlit. We were on our second beer when Ed leaned across the bar and said "Jessica's sister died today. I'm really glad you came along just now. She's needed somebody to talk to, to get her mind off of things."

For the first time on the bar tour, chit chat about local doings and statewide gossip fell away. No more carefree babble about our travels or questions about where we should head next. We stammered something to Ed and Jessica about how sorry we were, and listened numbly to the story of Jessica's sister in Casper, who just that day had succumbed to a health condition her family long knew she had.

I don't believe in the notion that things are "meant" to be. I don't believe that someone somewhere is intentionally getting us fired from jobs, or miscarrying pregnancies, or breaking up marriages. I believe that things just happen. It is how we take them up that makes us chose one fork of a river over another and sets the course for that moment of our life. But if I ever came close to believing in fate or luck, it was this moment. For us to have stumbled upon this bar was fairly remarkable by any standards of tourism navigation. And that we showed up just as Ed and Jessica returned from their trip for supplies to restock the bar really was a bit of luck.

If I were writing a piece of fiction, I couldn't have picked two better characters than us to enter the scene at that painful moment when they came back from town with enough provisions to sustain the bar while they were away at the funeral. If this were a story, the front door would swing open and in we'd step, full of merriment and conversation and news about doings in Laramie and Centennial. We'd keep talking for half an hour, filling up the time until some other friends in Granger could pick up their telephone message. They'd get the word about the death of Jessica's sister. They'd come over to the Cactus Tree Pub, worried, understanding, familiar faces at last, to help plan who would run the bar while Ed and Jessica made the trip to Casper to be with family. They would help make the decisions, while us sat quietly in the background. They knew who would help Jessica complete her large unfilled order of candles for a retail customer, which needed to be shipped right away. They knew who could run the cash register and handle the accounts. They knew who could handle the miners and oil rig workers who get a little rowdy sometimes, even though they usually left the bar before midnight to awaken at four a.m. for work. They knew who would take care of the itinerant sheep herders from Mexico, Peru and Chile who come to the bar for hamburgers and games of pool. Those men value their three-year work permits and their reliable employment on the big ranches of Wyoming and California, and they know better than to cause trouble.

I wish for Ed's and Jessica's sake none of these events had been real. But they were. I wish we would have offered to postpone the bar trip and stay on there, tending bar, flipping burgers, and shipping candles. They might have said yes. Fiction works that way, with things turning out in the most unlooked for ways. Small towns work that way, too, and it became apparent that the friend who was also the part time bartender and her family would be able to fill in where needed, like the Miracle-Gro planting soil, they'd been working with in their garden before they got the news. Where there had been sand and tired dirt in their Granger yard, tomatoes would be planted, nurtured by soft fertilized earth from a bag, a mixture good enough to send spindly green stems, hopeful yellow flowers, and red round globes of juicy determination out into the world. As strangers, we were there temporarily; we filled that space between putting the plant into the ground and dragging the hose over from the porch. We steadied the seedling, but the neighbors and friends were the soil, the water, and the sunlight.

We said goodbye to the bar company, exchanged email addresses, and made mutual offers of future visits.

Ed and Jessica sometimes come to Laramie for Wyoming Cowboy basketball games, so we'll look for their faces in the crowd at the arena come winter.

We got back in the car with the map and the dog and the cracker crumbs, and headed back to the highway to find our next group of future bar friends. But a piece of our spirits stayed behind in Granger, ready to rendezvous with ghosts of Mountain Men and Pony Express riders on the banks of the Blacks Fork, and with any other Wyomingites past or present who cared to join in.

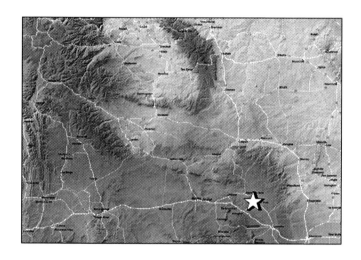

Fog on the Mountain, Professors in the Air
Double Shot Saloon
Rock River, Wyoming

The Double Shot is the only bar in Rock River, a town where one can also find a little café called the Pronghorn and one of the more modern and attractive rural K-12 schools in the state. I'd been in that school twice in my former job as a health educator with a local family planning service. I had been invited to talk with a handful of high school aged kids about the importance of guarding oneself from the unwelcome consequences of unprotected sex.

The students were attentive, mature, and polite. I'm not sure if my message got across in any long term behavior shaping sort of way. When something bad happens like a car accident or an earthquake, it is readily apparent. But how does one ever know when something bad is prevented, when stopping early at a yellow light takes you out of the range of a speeding train at a poorly marked railroad crossing? I'd reflected on this question often, including during both my visits to the Pronghorn over a patty melt and iced tea after visiting the school. I'd been tempted to stop in at the Double Shot after those lunches, but both times dutifully pointed my little brown hatchback south down Highway 30 and made the forty-five mile trip back to Laramie.

Finally, because of this bar tour, we made a point to stop at the Double Shot with two other people who'd also often driven by and idly thought they'd need to stop in there, one of these days. They were our friends Bob and Carolyn, whom we've known for several years through the University of Wyoming and other connections.

We have a lot in common with Bob and Carolyn. We live in the same neighborhood, we have similar cultural interests, we like a good bottle of wine. But they have something we don't have: a pool table in their basement. The Double Shot Bar has a pool table, of course, and our friends, in their confidence borne of practice, and we, relying on our shaky credibility as professional bar tourists, spent a good three hours playing a total of three very long doubles games. (The men defeated the women two out of three.) Since we were nearly the only customers in the bar on this Saturday afternoon, we didn't have to worry about monopolizing the pool table, or the jukebox, from which we solicited muffled tunes by Buffalo Springfield, Deep Purple, Jim Croce, and James Taylor.

Eventually, our beer and pool-induced jolliness helped us reduce the sometimes palpable gap between bar community regulars and drop-ins. After some ice-breaking conversation, we learned that the bartender on that day was filling in for the regular bartender, who in turn was painting the temporary bartender's house. The temporary bartender had had a stroke recently and wasn't getting around very well.

A woman named CJ was there, two packs of Marlboros stacked neatly on the bar in front of her like fresh decks of cards. CJ and the bartender, plus a customer named Dan, were talking about the importance of teaching young kids how to handle and shoot firearms. Dan had been in Vietnam and was describing his tour there, during which time he'd been shot three times. These adults, like many others, believe it is vital to teach kids the importance of protecting themselves from the unintended consequences of foolish behavior with guns. Who knows how many tragic accidents that approach will prevent in the local youth? Likely more than the converse approach of keeping kids in the dark, ignorant to the dangers that surround them.

In between pool games and chats with the bar regulars, the four of us rested at a little round table, pool cues across our knees, and talked about all the places in Wyoming and environs we meant to get to, one of these days. Bob has been to many small Wyoming towns over the years, mainly because his job, from which he'd recently retired, took him there. However, Carolyn stayed home during most of his business travels, because of her own commitments to her teaching job and the daily care of their children. She detailed a long list of places in Wyoming she'd like to see, from its larger towns to its scenic wild places. Like many Wyomingites, she's taken her vacations in warm, sunny places that provoke envy in those of us left behind in the wind and the blowing snow. However, after twenty years in this state she is ready to do what Ron and I have done with many of our Wyoming summers: drive around in big lazy circles, gawk up at mountain ranges, camp among coyotes and blue grouse, and meet people who happen into bars at the same time we do.

Bob's extensive Wyoming travels have an added dimension. Not only has he driven on every highway and nearly every byway in the state, he's also seen the state in bas relief: he's been airlifted to various towns as part of what I like to call the University of Wyoming's "flying professors" program. This endeavor went on for several years in the 1980s in the days before less dangerous forms of distance education, such as compressed video, became the norm. Bob tells stories about some harrowing but now amusing incidents (still not amusing to Carolyn) involving flights in bad weather, landing on airstrips with runway lights that seemed mere sparklers in the darkness. Like bags of rice or sugar, he and other scholars were dropped into "academically underserved" communities in the state to lead courses in the humanities. Who knows how many Wyoming citizens were better able to form useful beliefs about how to live a good and ethical life, as a result of these visits?

Like people everywhere, Wyomingites want to do the right things. They want their children to grow up healthy without anything encumbering their future before the time is right. They want to learn about how other people think and live, while still championing the independence implicit in a chiefly rural lifestyle. Like many people, they follow a system of belief to help them understand what "right" means. They trust that people working together in order to achieve common goals make good things happen. They know that unabated criminal behavior, from vandalism to robbery to corporate villainy, is the sort of thing best to prevent. They work to discourage bad things by teaching important lessons to their kids.

Like people all over the world, Wyomingites want answers to the why and how of life. Some people use religious faith to fill the gap between the how and the why, between the pull of a trigger and the bang of the gun. They say, "It is God's will," as explanation for the un-nuturing ways of the universe. Others say, "That's just the way it goes." Still others say, "If I had stayed and chatted with Bill for five extra seconds, that car that T-boned the guy behind me on the road would have hit me instead. I must be living right."

These types of questions were as palpable in the Double Shot as the click of pool balls and the hum of the beer cooler, that day of our visit. Just a few days before, there was a shocking and unexpected traffic accident on I-80 between Laramie and Cheyenne. During winter, icy roads and poor conditions not uncommonly lead to fatal wrecks. But this crash took place in the middle of August, in the middle of the day, a time no one would think something that bad would happen on the road. Instead, a thick blanket of fog had settled in over the highway, causing near-zero visibility and a chain-reaction collision that caught up thirty-seven vehicles. It was the fire that claimed several victims, including a woman from Rock River, along with her teenage son. If they'd decided against going to Cheyenne that day, they wouldn't have been involved. If they'd left Rock River two minutes earlier, they would have seen the collision in their rearview mirror instead of their windshield.

Local investigators spent several weeks measuring skid marks and forensic evidence to determine the "hows" of the accident. But that evening in Rock River, a fundraiser for the local volunteer fire department had coincidentally been scheduled. We attended, ate dinner and potluck desserts, and listened to the conversation around us. A couple of hundred people had shown up for the event, which became a combination VFD fundraiser and memorial service for the mother and son.

"How" questions and their explanations were in the air even while "why" shimmered unanswered. In fact, the bodies of the two from Rock River had not yet been positively identified by the medical examiner. Everyone just knew, in the information exchange of a community, that the victims were two of their own. At the community gathering that night, the healing was just beginning.

Maybe only a practiced bar tourist like me would find reconciliation between how and why questions on a book of matches at the Double Shot. I've since searched for the origin of this quote and only found what I already knew: the origin is unknown. *Let no one say and say it to your shame/ that all was Beauty here until you came.* That about sums it up.

Life is unpredictable, and predictable, wonderful and awful and over in a flash or after a long drawn out farewell. That saying means to me that whatever else you do, though, take care of your own dang self and don't mess things up for other people. To me, that is both the how and the why, rolled into a lozenge of common sense and hope. Could the flying professors coasting in the thin air of a Wyoming night, stars at their back and mountains at their feet, have put it any better?

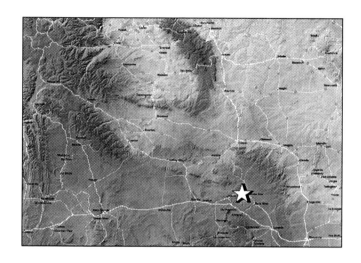

Time Travel
The Dip Bar
Medicine Bow, Wyoming

I ease back on the red velvet tufted high backed seat and squeeze my eyes mostly shut, letting in just enough light to make out the gear shift lever and the dashboard display indicating date month and year. As I tug the lever my eyes pop open wide, helpless against the G-force. Through the window near my seat, cloud covered days and moonlit nights whistle past like pictures in a flipbook. As I pull the lever closer and closer to my chest, a whirring sound arcs inside my head from one ear canal to the other and back again. I am nearly overcome by the sound, but I still notice the rise and fall of walls and buildings and forests and mountains, all close enough for me to reach out and touch. I don't waste my strength but instead focus on a unique consciousness of each atom in my body. My being vibrates in sympathetic pitch with the universe, somewhere in the space between C major and B.

I can't gauge how long I spend in this altered state, but finally I force myself to become aware of my external surroundings. The spinning date display shows the time is 140 million years before the present. I've reached the late Jurassic period, my destination. I focus my energy enough to lift one of my arms and push the gear lever straight back to stop. Abruptly, the whirring sound ceases, and my atomic-level body awareness is replaced by a reassuring sense of having intact arms, legs, head and a trunk. As I focus my vision, I notice that a great swampy lake and stand of conifers lies not far away from where I sit in my time machine. Between my position and the lake, a group of twenty-ton beasts feeds along the tops of the trees. Elongated necks. Ninety feet long. Whip-like tails. Diplodocus.

"Can I get you another Miller?" asks Bill the bartender. Bam. Just like that, I'm back on my green vinyl barstool, at the Diplodocus Bar in Medicine Bow, just a stone's throw from the Como Bluff dig site, one of the most renowned dinosaur graveyards in the world. The group of dinosaurs, the stand of conifers, and the swampy lake are still right over the hill, virtually close enough to smell. Except that they are way in the past, in the distant Jurassic. All we can see of them now are their fossilized remains, some of which have been carted away by paleontologists, and mounted in museums in places like New York City.

Everything about the tumbleweed town of Medicine Bow and the bar known locally as the Dip invites fantasies about different times. *Time Machine* author H.G. Wells never visited here, but his contemporary, Owen Wister, did. Wister wrote a novel that spawned a hotel which in turn birthed a frequently visited Western tourist destination, at least before the interstate came in and routed car travelers to the south.

Medicine Bow is the setting of Wister's novel *The Virginian: A Horseman of the Plains*, all about a cowboy from back East who comes West, leaving his name behind with his family in case he ever needs it again. He doesn't need it in the West, of course. All he needs is a strong horse, an honest day's work, and by golly, a good woman. Turns out he gets all three, after whomping some local smart-alecks, including one particularly annoying fellow named Trampas, target of that withering one-liner: "When you call me that, smile." Trampas has a motel in Medicine Bow named for him, too, but it isn't nearly as famous as The Virginian Hotel, itself.

The Virginian was published to wild popular acclaim in 1902, and lots of folks wanted to come through town and see where it all went down. The town fathers knew a good thing when they saw it and in 1909 started construction on the hotel bearing the title character's name. It opened to the public in 1911. Other Wister-themed tourist elements were promoted in town, such as the train station where the author spent a night sleeping on a makeshift bed while awaiting transportation to the nearby ranch where he was to spend the summer working, writing, and recovering from a nervous condition so frequent among sensitive Eastern types.

A display dedicated to Wister stands in the Medicine Bow Museum, just a stroll across the highway from the hotel. On the grounds of the museum, Owen Wister's hunting cabin also stands. It was moved there from its original location near Jackson Hole as part of Wyoming's statehood centennial celebration.

Wister wrote most of *The Virginian* after he returned to the East from his summer on the ranch. He visited Wyoming and stayed at the hunting cabin on a few occasions after that, but he didn't come back to Medicine Bow. Wister never saw the hotel he inspired, which in turn inspired so much Western cowboy mythology. But that mythology still puts Medicine Bow on the path of people on Old West tours, even though it means leaving divided highways behind and heading to southern Carbon County on one of Wyoming's lightly traveled and sometimes downright deserted two laners. Dizzyingly for Wyoming, tourism trends come and go, like the energy boom. But when Old West Mania hits an occasional dry spell, Medicine Bow has another card up its sleeve: Dinotourism.

Although the Como Bluff dig site is not open to the public, it is being studied by paleontologist from the University of Wyoming, the University of Montana, and other institutions, and folks like to see the area. The site was discovered in the 1870s by workers on the Union Pacific Railroad. Fossil finds from the area include dozens of species of dinosaur. Excavators discovered twenty-six new species, many with complete or nearly complete skeletons, and forty-five new species of Jurassic mammals. Five types of long necked herbivores were in the mix, along with other smaller herbivores and some carnivores, too. Just south of Medicine Bow on private property along the highway stands the Como Museum. It bills itself as the oldest building on earth. Probably true, since it is constructed entirely of dinosaur bones and other fossils found on the property. Although the museum's hours of operation are about as dependable as a mirage on this high dry plain, people still like to wander the nearby public lands looking for rocks to kick.

Maybe somewhere in those rocks and bones a dinosaur left the answer to the question that leaves paleontologist, science buffs, and little kids all over the world scratching their heads. No sooner had dinosaur remains been discovered than people began to look around and notice that no more of the creatures remained. Where did they go? The theories to explain their absence—asteroids, tsunamis, climate change, natural selection—all these explanations seem unsatisfying to our Q&A culture. What were these mysterious beings like? Were they constantly fighting and snarling and hurling one another off cliffs, like creatures in a Japanese monster movie?

Early answers to these questions have created myths about the creatures: that they were all huge, slow, dumb as dirt, and hunted on a regular basis by hairy guys in furry togas wielding billy clubs. Thank goodness Jurassic Park-induced dinomania came along and set us non-scientists straight on some key dates and times in the chronology.

Most dinosaurs evolved around 228 million years ago, and most were extinct sixty-five million years ago. Not all prehistoric animals were dinosaurs, and they didn't all evolve and extinguish in unison. They were gone before humans came along. Unfortunately, they are no more communicative to us now than the beds of rock and mud in which their fossilized remains are found. But there is something about seeing the imprint of an ancient creature's footprint, embedded in the mud and now exposed to modern eyes through accident or excavation, something that says a sentient being that way walked. That way will I walk. That way will I die. Will I take my fellow human beings with me, or will I go alone?

All that cosmic and karmic rock-kicking makes a dinomaniac thirsty. Luckily, Medicine Bow has two watering holes that serve good food to dinotourists and visitors of every ilk. Both the Dip and the Virginian Hotel get business from passing travelers and sportsmen, but the Dip, on the strength of its name alone, trades on dinosaurs and the geology of the area. Its bar top is made of a huge piece of jade mined not far from here. Jade is Wyoming's state mineral, not co-incidentally.

The Dip's proprietors, Bill and JoAnne, have created a comfortable establishment in the traditional Western mode. Bill is an accomplished craftsman whose work fills the building. Look up on the ceiling: painted there are images of Western characters and animals. Look on the walls, the table tops, the floors. Landscapes of the Medicine Bow area. Safely housed in locked glass cabinets are intricate representations of horses and wagons carved out of single pieces of ash or basswood. Bill, with aw-shucks Wyoming modesty, allows as how we probably can't afford his larger works, which he says sometimes take up to a year to carve. I'm sure he's got us pegged. JoAnne does her part in the décor department, too, and her handicrafts are on display throughout the multi-roomed bar and restaurant.

The time we spent in the Dip that day was necessarily short. So, we didn't play pool or have anything to eat more intricate than fried mozzarella sticks. But we sampled the beer (cold: we approved) and chatted with some of the other customers about the bar tour and such. This mid-August late afternoon outing came to a close, and we headed back south toward Laramie, over the gently rolling yellow hills dotted with antelope and ancient rock formations. Our Toyota RAV4 is no time machine but at least for comfort and convenience it beats the covered wagons of earlier Wyoming voyagers. As we drove we were on high alert, scanning the vegetation along the roadside for prairie dogs considering a dart onto the highway. We urged the ones we spotted back to safety with a toot of the car horn.

If I had stopped my imaginary time machine in this same spot a thousand years ago, I might have met groups of native people moving among hunting grounds along the Medicine Bow River. If I'd have stopped two hundred years ago, I might have met those same people's descendants having some of their early encounters with Europeans. A hundred years ago I might have had a chance to try out my theory of Toyota vs. Conestoga. Seventy-five years ago I might have met some of the earliest automobile traffic making its way up U.S. 30, en route to Yellowstone National Park.

But with a forward rather than backward nudge on the lever, I could see the future. One year from now maybe I'd find myself again on that same barstool, talking to Bill and JoAnne and the locals who join their society. Maybe we'd be talking about how Wyoming should invest its mineral wealth surplus. Maybe we'd share stories about antelope hunts, undertaken with guns or cameras. Maybe Bill would have taken it into his head to carve a jackalope, recently named Wyoming's official mythological creature. Perhaps we'd sip from one of the Dip's coffee mugs, featuring a cartoon image of the dinosaurs that in extinction are as powerful as any myth. That comfortable scene would be enough to entice me to take the spark plugs out of the time machine, clamp a parking boot on one of its wheels, throw its ignition keys down a prairie dog hole, and spend forever in the land of dinosaur graveyards, dusty cowboy heroes, and Wyoming artists working in oil, wood, and good company.

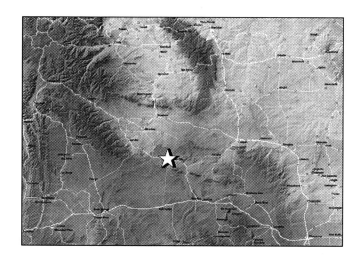

Bikes Along the Bar Trail
Split Rock Bar, Jeffrey City, Wyoming
&
Sweetwater Station, Wyoming

Split Rock Bar

Sweetwater Station

Along the shoulder of U.S. 287, just west of Muddy Gap Junction, a bicyclist pulling a Burley trailer pumps toward the Wind River Mountains, which are not yet visible on the horizon but are attested to by the highway map. The trailer provides substantial drag against the smart Wyoming headwind. The bicyclist is a young man dressed in lycra togs and a neckerchief. His thighs operate in perpetual motion, ignoring what his mind must be telling him about distance past and distance yet to come. All angled arms and legs and rounded wheels, the rig is a mobile on a mission.

We pull safely five feet to the left as we approach in our car to give the cyclist plenty of room, not concerned about oncoming traffic because there is none—from either direction. This stretch of road between Muddy Gap Junction and our destination at Sweetwater Station is lonely, even in August during the height of summer travel season. Even lonelier is Wyoming Highway 135, which cuts north out of Sweetwater Station toward the Wind River Indian Reservation. On that road you could safely give your fifteen year-old his first driving lessons. In a stick. Unlike learning in a supermarket parking lot, here he'd be unlikely to hit anything.

Soon the cyclist shrinks in our review mirror and becomes just another curiosity along the road. We're looking forward to stopping at the Split Rock Bar and Café in Jeffrey City. We've driven this road a hundred times between us but have never stopped in at the bar in this quasi ghost town. Ghost towns aren't just relics of nineteenth century gold mining frenzies. They rise and fall on the Western plains with the speed and certainty of a spring squall that dumps wet snow from the sky, already melting as it piles.

Jeffrey City was built from the rock and sand of the desert when uranium mining was going to power the whole country. That was in the 1950s, and the town was rockin'. Eventually it boasted four bars, a new K-12 school with a huge gymnasium, two gas stations, and a store. Now those places sit with boards for windows. After a few nuclear power plant accident scares in the 1980s, the enthusiasm for uranium sagged and workers took their families and followed the money to the next sure fire thing of the future.

But they left behind a "town drunk and a town nut," according to the Split Rock's bartender. The former had just been "eighty-sixed from the bar," the bartender explained, and the latter left soon after we arrived. She inexplicably hates all people from Laramie, it turns out. But the bartender seemed happy company for us as we settled into our spots and talked more local history.

The town was once called Home on the Range, but was renamed for Dr. Charles W. Jeffrey, one of the biggest cheerleaders for the uranium ore in the nearby Crooks Gap and Gas Hills. Jeffrey City was a company town of the Western Nuclear Company, which turned the uranium ore into yellow cake that was then shipped elsewhere for further refining.

The Split Rock Bar and Café was named for a huge rip in the rock of the Rattlesnake Range to the east. That split forms a landmark visible for a hundred miles. Like a geologic billboard, it guided emigrants along the Oregon Trail to the stage station at its feet. There travelers could find refreshment along the Sweetwater River. Today that huge split in the rock is mostly ignored by car-cloaked travelers who have their directions spelled out for them by AAA or by in-car global positioning systems. Even bicyclists with Burleys have a pretty good idea of where they are going, but for those of us who like to stop along the road, the rest area and picnic tables and especially the outhouses are a mighty fine find.

The bartender at Split Rock told us a story illustrating how the remoteness of a place like Jeffrey City necessitates trust in its inhabitants and even passers by.

A recent customer, a stranger, had car trouble, and the bartender let the customer take her truck about sixty miles round trip to the nearest auto parts store.

The customer couldn't believe she'd trusted him with her vehicle. "What else was he going to do?" she asked. "Nobody was going to come out here and help him." Besides, she got twenty dollars of gas money out of the deal, although she tried to refuse the payment. As Ron and I pondered the distance/trust continuum, the door opened and in from the bright sunshine stepped the young man from the bicycle-Burley rig. He'd finally caught up with us; he, the turtle, getting acquainted with each rolling tumbleweed; we, the rabbits, getting to the bar fast, clean, but not thirsty enough to truly deserve the cold beer we were served.

The young man clicked across the orange and white paleo-linoleum floor, his bike-shoe cleats clacking tile instead of clamping pedal. "Sorry about these shoes. They sure are loud" he apologized, by way of ice-breaking. "I can't take them off. They're the only shoes I have."

He hopped on to the barstool next to me—sprightly considering the exhausting ride against the wind. He introduced himself as Rex and said he was on a solo bike ride across the country. He'd started in Michigan, where he was attending college and studying natural resource management. He hopes to "do something with fish." One day he thinks he'll probably go to graduate school or the Peace Corps. But for now he was riding across America, sleeping where he could, eating what he could, living off the fat of his credit card limit. Unfortunately, he hadn't reckoned on places like the Split Rock Bar and Café that didn't take plastic.

We'd just asked for menus when Rex arrived and were debating between the Indian taco and the buffalo burger. Rex asked for water as we sipped our beers. Fumbling in the dark places of his biking togs, Rex produced a handful of change and assorted greasy nuts and screws. He hemmed and hawed and stared unseeing at his menu. Long moments went by. The bartender waited, pencil poised above pad.

"You look hungry. Let us buy you lunch," we declared, finally sensing his discomfort and riding to the rescue. "Order what you want." It felt good to be magnanimous to a future Peace Corps-ite. We were drinking beer without really being thirsty, ordering Indian tacos without really being Indian. Why not buy the boy a grilled cheese? Sure, maybe he had a wad of cash somewhere stashed in the Burley outside and was just scamming us out of five dollars. Big deal. Travelers help one another out along the road in Sweetwater country. It's a tradition.

After we finished our lunches and beverages we said goodbye to the bartender and walked outside to the parking lot with Rex. We took a few photos and said our farewells, all planning to head in the direction of the Wind River Mountains. We were going to stop first at the next bar, about twenty miles up the road at Sweetwater Station, and he was hoping to make Lander, another forty miles, before dark. After we motored past trying not to spray him with parking lot gravel, we all heliotroped toward the sinking sun; he, moving with the geologic slowness that split Split Rock; we, moving with the power of carbon burning in our engine.

Maybe it was the heat or the beer, but as we headed toward the next stop my imagination started to run away with me. I considered it too bad that no one ever thought of powering a two-wheeled vehicle in a way that would allow it to burn fuel, not need pedaling, and go very fast. An internal combustion engine powering rubber wheels—that would be just the thing.

Sounds like the sort of thing the Germans should look into. I could almost picture it—two-wheeled motor bikes zooming the highways, small enough that they could ride side by side. Of course, at those speeds, bugs would be a problem. Maybe the bikes could have some sort of windshield attached, like an automobile has. Riders would need protective gear in case of a crash. Maybe leather worn over regular clothes would do the trick. Naturally, riders would love to form clubs, and organize races and rallies. Thousands of enthusiasts would attend, and there would be pig roasts, and concerts, and contests for the best motorcycle. Edgar Winter would be in demand as a musical performer, playing rock-based blues music on his keyboards or alto sax, long white hair hanging over his black leather jacket, brushing against sew-on patches he'd been given at rallies sponsored by Harley Davidson and ...wait a minute... what's this up ahead on the left? Looks like a 1920s era rambling white building, with a gas station, a little market, and a bar. Parked in front are several of the conveyances

I just described. Could Edgar Winter fans be living it up there, inside Sweetwater Station?

Distance in Wyoming has a way of lubricating the imagination, like spray WD-40 on a stubborn lock. And time has a way of being tangible, with moments that stack like the minerals that formed the earth. Between Jeffrey City and Sweetwater Station, geologic events, early man, historic pioneer travels, bike trails, bar tours, all take chalky dry shape and stack up along both sides of the highway. Those chunks of time at the topmost level stud themselves with sagebrush and cactus. Through it all flows the Sweetwater River. Along it travel cars, and trucks, and bicycles, and yes, motorcycles.

Travelers today barely notice the modest little Sweetwater River, easily forded by bridges that one hardly notices in a car. But back when people traveled this area under human power, they were grateful for the first water for many miles around that wasn't loaded with alkali. They may have thought the meandering river wore out its welcome just a bit, however. Anyone in a hurry would eventually cross it nine times in order to move efficiently in a more or less straight line toward destinations to the west.

If anyone deserved a cold beer on a hot afternoon, it would have been those pioneer travelers—just the very people for whom such refreshment would have been an impractical indulgence. Therefore, we considered it our duty to our pioneer ancestors to make a good showing of ourselves at the Sweetwater Station bar. In we stepped to meet third generation Sweetwater Station owners Mattie and Rick, and their biker friends Jeff and Allen.

Jeff runs a motorcycle customizing shop in Lander. Burly and T-shirted, it would be hard to imagine him in any other profession, except possibly rock concert promoter. Turns out he's that, too. He's found a way to combine his loves of biking and rock music by helping stage poker runs that climax in a big party, complete with live music and overnight camping. A poker run involves organizing a bunch of bikers to pay a bit of money and then ride a set route, stopping at participating bars. Bikers have a drink and pick up a playing card at each stop, and by the end they have a selection of cards they hope will be the winning hand.

Jeff told us about one of these events he'd organized recently, when he'd had the good fortune to book the aforementioned Edgar Winter as the main attraction for the post-run concert. Edgar Winter is no stranger to these sorts of gigs. He performs regularly at world famous biker events such as the Harley Davidson Rally in Sturgis, South Dakota. His appearance at the local poker run was quite the coup for Jeff.

Turns out the event was one Jeff won't soon forget. During the concert, confusion ensued around a drum set that was to either be shared between the opening band and Edgar's, or not shared and removed from the stage between sets: No one knew for sure and that's what caused the problem. Tempers flared up between Jeff and Edgar Winter's road manager, and for awhile, it appeared Edgar's band would refuse to perform. Eventually, Jeff was led before Edgar, he of the flowing albino-white hair and sled-dog blue eyes. Jeff describes the conversation as one whose outcome could have gone either way.

"Edgar Winter chewed my ass," he says, with a mixture of pride and humility. After all, how many people can say that? After Jeff "humbled" himself in front of a lot of people, Edgar agreed to play and everyone had a great time. Undaunted by that run in, Jeff is planning another poker run and concert event for a future Labor Day weekend.

Meanwhile, on this afternoon Jeff was with his friend Allen at Sweetwater Station. Allen is a photographer and documentary film maker from Las Vegas. He's also a bike aficionado, and that's why he came to Lander the previous summer and happened to meet Jeff.

Allen and a small crew had been making a documentary film about the Sturgis rally, and stopped in Lander at the custom bike shop where they had every expectation of finding leather-clad folks on their way to the big party. Allen asked if Jeff and his shop workers would help him get film footage by pretending to be on their way to Sturgis. Allen planned to film the preparations and get a bit of live riding action for his documentary. Jeff and his workers didn't want to go through all that fuss in order to pretend to go somewhere. They had a better idea. So they saddled up the Harleys and went for a real ride out to Sweetwater Station.

Allen had such a good time with Jeff and company that he arranged to spend some time with the gang when he came out for the next years' Sturgis rally. That's what he was doing at the Station when Ron and I stopped in on the bar tour.

Ron brought his camera in to take some interior shots, and Allen had his camera, too. Inevitably, camera tech-talk broke the ice, and soon we were all pals. Mattie allowed Spike to come in from the car, and Allen told us all about his girlfriend's Pomeranian back home. Spike wandered into the market part of the Station and located, with the unfailing nose of a truly spoiled pet, the Kit Kat bars on a low shelf. I wandered in to the market and stopped him from cleaning out the supply.

We all enthused about how much we liked the music of Edgar Winter. Ron told a story about sitting a few rows ahead of Edgar and his entourage on an airplane, but not asking for an autograph. Jeff and Allen just shook their heads.

We told them all about the bar tour. We said to expect a goofy kid on a bike, the slow kind (the bike, not the kid), who might be showing up here in a couple more hours. They shook their heads again and wondered about the crazies from Back East. Turns out this highway is near several trails popular with cyclists, many of whom stop to rest on highway pullouts, dazed and exhausted, like lycra-clad prophets who know that doom is coming, but forget when.

Eventually it was time for us to head to Lander for the night, so we all walked outside to the parking lot and took several group and individual photos of one another. Jeff and Allen had just visited the bar we were headed to the next day, the Union in Hudson, and said it was lots of fun with accordion music and free cabbage rolls to celebrate a regular patron's eighty-third birthday. We were sad to say goodbye to our new friends, but the next bar sounded enticing enough to soften the blow.

Lots of people have said hello and goodbye to one another in this exact spot, even before the Sweetwater Station was established in 1862. It was a telegraph relay station, a military supply base, and a Pony Express Station, until the military ceased protecting it from Indian skirmishes in 1866 and left it to its own devices. But Rick and Mattie's predecessors knew a good location, and established the gas station in 1926. It is a long way into Lander for supplies, whether in a car, on a motorcycle, riding a bicycle, a wagon, a horse, or proceeding on foot. It wouldn't be a surprise to see any of these conveyances along the route, stacked up in time, shimmering in the hot afternoon air.

Rendezvous? Bring it On!
Jim Bridger Club
Ft. Bridger, Wyoming

*Rendezvous—Noun: a meeting arranged
for a specified time and place; the location
of a prearranged meeting; a popular meeting
place for people. Verb: to meet, or meet somebody,
at a specified time and place, or cause this
to happen.*

The time is somewhere between 1825 and 1840. Raggedy white men who smell of blood and gunpowder spend months in the mountains, trapping and skinning beaver for pelts for the fur trade business. Every so often, a man has to come down out of those hills, sell pelts, buy more goods, socialize with fellow trappers, eat and drink too much, and maybe get lucky with a neighborly woman and possibly even marry her. So every year they arrange a time and place to meet: thus was born the Mountain Man Rendezvous. Several of these multi-day parties were held at various spots in the Green River Valley of southwest Wyoming, just one valley over from where Jim Bridger would found the trading post that became Ft. Bridger. Eventually Bridger would have a bar named after him, which figures as not the least of his legendary accomplishments as a mountain man and military scout, before his death 1881, when he was seventy-seven.

Jim Bridger opened his trading post along the Oregon Trail in 1843, selling much needed goods to westward travelers. After a few years, trail travel petered out past his place when faster routes west were found. Bridger eventually settled a hard-fought feud with Mormon leader Brigham Young that involved fires and gun battles, and sold the facility to the Mormons. The trading post became a Mormon colony in 1855, then a military outpost in 1858. Now it is a mostly restored historic site interpreting the emigrant experience for history buffs and modern day Mountain Man Rendezvous re-enactors. Fort Bridger is also a town, where about four hundred people dwell in the shadows of the old fort. The town is one of a cluster of communities in Bridger Valley in Wyoming's southwestern-most county, Uinta. What is now a mixed landscape of arable plain and high sage-covered desert was once a moist meadowland popping with cottonwood trees. Before the influx of white trappers, emigrants, and the military, nomadic Native Americans benefited from the plentiful water in the streams that were fed by seasonal melt from the high Uinta Mountains, just to the south.

Archeologists have documented environmental changes in the Valley prompted by whites who weren't nomadic and needed a steady supply of ready food. They drained the meadows and irrigated land to grow crops and graze animals. Their reshaping of the environment has largely held to this day.

Historic site visitation is the main tourist draw to the area, which is about three miles off Interstate 80. The Jim Bridger Club is reputed locally to be one of the classier bars in the valley, which made it a dandy rendezvous spot for us and several other bar tourists on a fine June evening. The beige-and-brick building sits about two blocks down the road from the Ft. Bridger State Historic Site. A sign on the side of the structure proclaims "Jim Bridger Club Bar Liquor Store." A modern trading post if ever there was one.

All of us in the bar were taking time off from something, but maybe not as much in need of a break as the early mountain men. The bartender was working at the club because a concussion from a trona mining accident had given him dizzy spells and headaches and made him change livelihoods. An off duty bartender was relaxing on a barstool, having a few cocktails now that her shift was over and she could unwind. Before the evening was over she would tip backwards off her tall stool and land flat on her back. She bounced back up, laughing. A couple folks hung out in the room off the bar, with an off duty woodstove and a pool table that was rarely vacant. A few working men were having a drink and a smoke before heading home to families and dinner. Another man came in, gulped two quick shots of tequila and bought a case of beer to go, which he carried out on his shoulder, all the while talking on his cell phone. A woman came in by herself later in the evening, getting away from what I wasn't sure. But either through experience or osmosis from being a local, she knew a great deal about the mining business, which had become a focus of our conversation.

I know embarrassingly little about mining, even though it has a significant impact, economically, environmentally, and culturally, on life in Wyoming. According to the Wyoming Mining Association, twenty-two mining companies operate fifty different mines around the state, digging like badgers for trona, bentonite, coal, and even uranium. The mining industry directly employed close to eight thousand people in the state during 2003. This figure doesn't include the number of people working in the oil and gas industry, which is also huge and growing huger. Royalties the mining companies pay have helped make Wyoming one of the few states in the nation operating in the black. Mining in Uinta and adjacent Sweetwater County, home of many of the big trona operations, provides steady employment and respectable wages. There is a downside to mining operations. Those jobs and wages are subject to booms and busts with variations in the national and world economy. Local and county governments don't flourish when workers are laid off, which means fewer services and fewer taxpaying residents. There are also environmental impacts as mining companies poke, gouge, or tear large holes in the earth to claim their material of choice.

If you look at a mining map of Wyoming, you'll see large trona deposits in the southeast. You'll see bentonite, mostly in the north central. You'll see uranium in the center of the state. You'll see coal deposits across a vast section of Wyoming.

Vast, but not all-encompasing. In Albany County, where my town of Laramie sits, there's no significant mining. As a result, Albany is one of the poorest counties in the state. Not only is there no mining revenue, but the main business in the county, the University of Wyoming, is tax exempt.

There has long been discussion in the legislature and other governmental bodies that it might be equitable to distribute mining money more or less evenly to all the counties, not just the ones sitting on top of a wealth of minerals. The state uses the money in ways they hope will benefit all the citizens, for example socking much of it away in a Permanent Mineral Trust Fund, drawing only the interest. By divvying more money up to the counties, everyone in the state could benefit from what the state itself possesses. But like all raging arguments, this one is complicated because there are a lot of sound points to the contrary.

One of those points was explained to us by a woman named Tammy, whom we met in the Jim Bridger Club. She and her husband lived in Laramie for many years, where they attended college and started their professions. They were on a bar tour of sorts, too, stopping into the Jim Bridger Club for the first time on their way home to Rock Springs, where they'd moved because of her husband's job in—what else—the mining industry.

The town of Rock Springs is a growing one, with close to twenty thousand residents. The boom in mining, and in oil and gas production, has caused the population to jump in recent years. Rock Springs is no stranger to this sort of rapid growth. In the boom period of the 1980s a similar thing happened, just before the big bust. Rock Springs was left with empty houses and empty schools. Even the ground began to collapse as coal mines under the town suspended operation and left hollow pockets under the topsoil and sand. Rock Springs was left dry, dusty, pockmarked, and with the reputation as the armpit of Wyoming. But a respectable community college, founded in 1966, and a proud history as an ethnically diverse Western railroad town, kept the population of regulars there hanging on.

Tammy and her husband had their doubts about leaving Laramie, where winter may last until June but at least rattlesnakes aren't hiding under every back porch. But now she says they've learned to love Rock Springs. She makes no secret of the fact that the economic boom that made her husband's job there possible is also responsible for the rising crime rate in town, and other social problems that come with an itinerant workforce of well paid unattached men with time on their hands after a long shift in the mine. Tammy and her husband used to believe that mineral wealth should be distributed to areas without mining, such as Albany County. At least, they believed that when they lived in Laramie. But now they argue that the people who have to put up with the negative effects of mining are the ones who deserve the financial compensation.

Like many people around the state, Tammy has a cheerful attitude about mining, or any other endeavor that puts money into people's pockets. She even takes the increased crime with a sense of humor. She talks about taking a trip down Elk Street in Rock Springs, the main drag through town where notorious activities take place, demanding of the area "let's see what you got." I asked if she was looking for a glimpse of drugs and violence. "And prostitution!" she added with enthusiasm. "Bring it on!"

Back in tiny Ft. Bridger, about eighty miles to the west of Rock Springs, things are a bit quieter. True, the motel down the block from the club, where we stayed the night, is inhabited partially by mine workers who rent rooms by the month, and start their diesel pickup trucks at four a.m. just to hear them run for an hour before they leave for the job. This I know from unhappy experience. But in general, Bridger Valley is a quiet, stable community that harbors working families and offspring who, if they go to college, will very possibly be the first in their family to do so. Neighboring towns of Lyman and Mountain View are within six miles of one another, and several unincorporated communities fill in the other blank spots. Together the towns form a jumping off spot to get away from the pressures of the boom and bust world and to plan a trip into the mountains, rivers, valleys and wildlife that attracted humans long before the days of Jim Bridger and the Mountain Men. But be careful of the moose. One knocked a woman off her motorcycle a few miles from Ft. Bridger as she rode by one day. That was a rendezvous she'll likely not soon forget.

The Sun and the Wind
Steelman's Bright Spot
Hiland, Wyoming

Drivers along U.S. 20/26 between Casper and Shoshoni can't help notice Steelman's Bright Spot, the only structure for twenty miles along this high plains highway. The one-story white building sits just outside striking distance of the Big Horn Mountains to the north, the Wind River Mountains to the west, and the Rattlesnake Range to the south. All these geographical points hold the promise of adventure, but each is distant enough that getting there takes some doing. In spite of the distances, the folks at Steelman's Bright Spot have plenty of company. Some of bar owners Bob and Carla's closest neighbors include amateur musicians and the rattlesnakes who reside down the road at a rocky geological feature descriptively called Castle Gardens. Not that these two groups are kin, but both are a prominent part of life at Steelman's Bright Spot.

The Bright Spot is the town of Hiland, population ten, elevation 5998, according to that most reliable of references, the bar T-shirt. The bar and its gas pumps hold on tight to the high plains where wind fills the sky and uranium fills the ground. People might know the territory if they are familiar with John McPhee's *Rising from the Plains*, which tells about the geology of Wyoming as mapped by native son J. David Love. Dr. Love was the son of a Scottish sheep rancher named John D. Love, whose spread covered much of the territory southwest of where the Bright Spot now stands, just south of Moneta and west of Hiland, on Muskrat Creek.

People may be familiar with the Love family through the book *Lady's Choice*, a collection of letters edited by Barbara Love and Frances Love Froidevaux, daughters of J. David and Jane Love, with a foreword by John McPhee. The book includes letters between John D. Love and his future wife, Ethel Phoebe Waxham. Miss Waxham taught for one year at the Mills family ranch school, on the eastern flank of the Wind River Mountains. By standards of rural life in 1905, that made John Love and the Mills family, along with Miss Waxham, neighbors. That neighborliness sparked a five-year courtship during which the pair regularly corresponded, even after Miss Waxham left Wyoming for other pursuits. In 1910 they married, settled at the ranch on Muskrat Creek, and had a family that would include the famed geologist.

Rural standards of proximity and neighborliness haven't changed much in these hundred years. Ranches still take up a lot of room, and they don't run themselves.

Many ranch families live quite happily in homes miles from the nearest neighbor. But just because people like some elbow room doesn't mean they don't need companionship. Just as the Loves, the Mills, and other rural families visited each other's ranches for dances and holidays regardless of the hardships of travel, so people today occasionally gravitate to social crossroads like the Bright Spot.

On this day of the bar tour we'd been planning to visit the Tumble Inn at Powder River, not far from Casper. We arrived on a Thursday afternoon in April and found the place locked up but with a sign explaining that exotic dancers took the stage every "Wed thru Sat" from eight p.m. to midnight. A new development in this bar, which I'd been very excited to visit based on the twice life-sized neon cartoon cowboy that rises high above the plains from the Tumble Inn's loosely demarked parking lot. The development didn't make me happy. I realize that it's a living, and there may be lots of paying customers willing to finance the exotic dance trade, especially with the state's boom in temporary, unattached male energy workers. But we wanted a cold beer and a chance to interact with bar customers, not to be faced with a stage show that wouldn't leave much space for conversation. Besides, the first pasty wouldn't twirl for several more hours, so down the road we went, toward the next promising spot on the map.

We'd heard of the bar at Hiland from some folks in Laramie, so were looking forward to discovering whether the place was as much fun as rumored. We were surprised

to be confronted with a bar so small one of Mr. Love's
sheep wagons would have seemed roomy by comparison.
The potential fun wasn't simply concentrated in this one
part of the building, however. A convenience store took up
most of the square footage of the place. In addition to
travel necessities, the store offered just about everything
one could dream up to make from rattlesnake skin.
Wallets, keychains, knife sheaths, and other objects
reminded us of the resident of that range to the south. In
fact, the bar folks told us that just the day before our visit,
snake hunters had gone into Castle Gardens and scooped
up hibernation-groggy rattlers just emerging from their
dens, and had brought them by the bar for show and tell.
Castle Gardens might be a less rattle-y spot as a result of
this reptile repurposing, but never safe enough for people
who hike or horseback ride in this country and would
rather not be kissed by a poisonous snake.

There isn't much snakeskin in the bar itself
because the walls and ceilings are covered with business
cards, bumper stickers, and photos of hunts successful
from the point of view of the predator, at least. We could
have spent our time reading these missives tacked to the
walls, and never have talked to anyone. But that wouldn't
be the Bar Tour Way. Instead, a conversational opening
presented itself almost immediately.

Behind the bar a woman named Pat filled in for the
owner, Bob, who was resting up from a long trip to Boise
and back. Pat's mother was visiting from Oklahoma, and
sat on the stool closest to us. Beyond her sat an oil
worker from Thermopolis named Phil, and beyond him, a

Hiland area local named Bill. (Carla herself was minding the store.)

The group was conversing about live music in the bar. I happen to be a regular abuser of a Fender acoustic guitar, and also frequently throttle my accordion, piano, and autoharp. I fancy myself a sought-after conversational partner on all subjects musical, so I jumped right in with questions, clamors, and exclamations. Turns out after just a few minutes of insinuating myself into the party, I was challenged to put my fingers where my mouth was and was handed the Bar Guitar.

Remember the scene in *Coal Miner's Daughter*, where Loretta Lynn, played by Sissy Spacek, gives her first performance in a redneck-filled honky-tonk? She'd been writing songs at home for the kids until her husband had the idea she might make some money singing her songs in public and recording them. I think I know how Loretta might have felt. Heck, I can play guitar all night long at home by myself or with a few familiar friends. I even have a little group I jam with, called the Write Tones because many of us are writers of various sorts. But here I was in this tiny bar, perched high on a stool in a section of the floor elevated above the rest. Eerily like a stage.

Phil handed me up the Bar Guitar and the crowd of five got semi-quiet. They talked amongst themselves enough that I didn't imagine too bright a spotlight on my forehead. But they were attentive enough that I had to sing and play something I at least knew the words to. Dwight Yoakum came to the rescue, and out popped a shaky version of *The Distance Between You and Me*.

No one threw beer bottles at me when I stopped. There was even a little nodding and applause. Another round for everyone. More songs. Then Phil played a few tunes. He's a songwriter and oil worker, trying to break into Nashville (not as an oil worker). He's written a song about his grandson called *My Little Buddy*, of which he's made a demo recording. He declares that soon he "will be noticed in Nashville," and we'll all be hearing about him there before too much longer.

After a few trades of the Bar Guitar, Phil and I had both played several songs. Bill looked on proudly. He is the owner of the Bar Guitar. Although he does not play any instruments, Bill collects guitars, amplifiers and recording equipment. He explains that he collects them because he just likes them. I think I found my biggest, possibly only fan, in Bill. Each song I played prompted a flurry of applause from him, and a new plan to stay at the Bright Spot a bit longer and have another beer and another bowl of pretzels to soak it up with. I began to appreciate the exotic dancers down the road, and how a minimally competent performance could seem, under the right circumstances, like an act straight from Carnegie Hall. And like exotic dancers, I'd discovered a new power in me to drive men to drink, though probably for different reasons. After all, no one was stuffing bills in the waistband of my relaxed fit Kmart bluejeans.

Musical prognostication filled the space between the songs Phil or I offered to the group. Phil is one of those musicians who knows the start of just about every pop and country song recorded between 1965 and 1987. I know the type, because I am one of them, too. So we'd each met our match in the other as he'd play the first few notes of a song on the Bar Guitar and I'd blurt out the title. It was like shooting musical clay pigeons. Pull! Plunk plunk twang. *La Bamba!* Pull! Twang plink plunk. *Stairway to Heaven!* Pull! Plink twang plunk. *Tea for the Tillerman!* More applause from Bill. More pretzels all around.

Eventually we ran out of songs and it was time for Bill to head home which was, fortunately for his driving record and other travelers on the highway, just up a side road a short distance. We needed to head back to Casper, but with regrets for leaving this place that certainly did live up to its billing for fun. Before we left, we purchased a bar T-shirt and asked Phil to autograph it, against the day he becomes a Successful Nashville Songwriter. I wish him the best but don't have much hope, not because of his talent but because of the character of the music industry. It doesn't pay to be original in the world of commercial country music. I, too, am hoping to become an SNS and took a less-than-dazzling fourth place in a contest I entered with my songwriting partner. Predictably, not much has come of it. I might have more luck in my show business career as a Wyoming novelty act. Maybe I could get a gig back down the road at the Tumble Inn. I could tape pasties to the body of my guitar, sing *Summer Breeze* by Seals and Croft, and set the pasties spinning like bawdy windmills. I could make creative uses of the snakeskin guitar strap I received as a prize in that songwriting contest, and give the Castle Garden snake hunters yet another idea. Who needs Nashville when we have our own bright spots right here in Wyoming?

The Rain and the Flood
Hole in the Wall Bar & Invasion Bar
Kaycee, Wyoming

Hole in the Wall

Invasion Bar

In the town of Kaycee two bars stand, one more than most towns included on this Wyoming bar tour. The two bars of Kaycee are inextricably connected, having stood side by side for many years until a flood sent the Hole in the Wall Bar drifting north along Nolan Avenue, leaving its companion, the Invasion Bar, with nothing but a hole in the ground for company.

A stubborn thunderstorm developed on August 26, 2002, and stalled over southern Johnson County, where Kaycee is located. Six hours later, the rain prompted the Middle Fork of the Powder River to leave its banks in downtown Kaycee and, according to NOAA, contributed to the dismemberment of "nineteen trailers, twenty-two houses, and twelve of Kaycee's fifteen businesses." The NOAA report describes the scene: "One hotel was broken in three pieces, with one piece carried seventy-five yards, and the other two pieces deposited a few hundred yards away on the opposite side of the Middle Fork of the Powder River." After the water receded and things dried out, the Hole in the Wall Bar found temporary digs down the road. Now it is housed in a remodeled gas station about a quarter mile away from its old friend, the Invasion.

I have a rough idea of how the people in those nineteen trailers and twenty-two houses might have felt when their world washed away in the early hours of August 27th. I've never lived through a flood, but many of my childhood midnights were disturbed by a flashlight shining in my face, with a parent on the other end of it shaking me from my dreams. Howling wind and sirens accompanied the words, "Tornado Warning! We have to go to the neighbors' right now!" My parents weren't fatalists like some veterans of Tornado Alley I knew, who would shrug their shoulders at the sound of the siren and say, "If it gets me, it gets me." Maybe because my parents had children they hoped to raise to adulthood, they took those warnings seriously.

Our family's post-war tract home on a dead end street was one of several on the block that sat on a concrete slab. The neighbors whose houses had basements would throw open the doors to us weather refugees until the sirens stopped. Those events were impromptu come-as-you-are parties for the adults who, in robes and slippers, would unfold the card table and then pry the lids off bottled beer with a church key, laughing above the sound of the transistor radio that broadcast the weather reports. We kids would cluster together over a board game and send our pieces up chutes and down ladders by flashlight. Some of those tornado parties were so fun we were disappointed when the siren stopped. Maybe that's because no tornados hit, at least not on our snug block that always seemed a safe harbor.

I've seen tornado devastation in other places and was curious to see the cleanup after the Kaycee flood. I wanted to visit both its bars, each named for events in the late nineteenth century: The Hole in the Wall Bar, for the spot where Butch Cassidy and other outlaws passed some time between heists, and the Invasion Bar, in honor of the Johnson County Wars, fought by factions of cattlemen and homesteaders over prime grazing land in Johnson County and environs.

Ron, Spike, and I left Laramie at six a.m., not in a tornado, but in a virtually blinding spring blizzard. The snow and icy roads eased up about an hour outside of town, at a spot that is normally only a half-hour outside of town. When we arrived in Kaycee late that afternoon we finally understood how significantly most of its manmade features had been rearranged by the flood—in a town of 250 residents we couldn't for the life of us locate our RV park. We found the next best thing, the Invasion, which was still snuggly where it was before the flood.

We walked in during a conversation between several bar customers and Amanda, the owner. They were poring over a local telephone book, trying to remember the middle name of a certain woman so they could find her number and call her up. One man kept pointing out that the woman was known to be at the post office, just up the street, and why didn't they just go up there and talk to her. I had a feeling that conversation might have been going on for hours or even days.

That's what happens with time in bars, especially Western bars, and most especially Wyoming bars. The space between Wyoming towns and the intervening basins and ranges and hoodoos and alfalfa fields make us understand viscerally what the physicists tell us: that time is not a straight line. I confess that everything I know about physics I've learned from Doctor Who and his universe-trekking Police Call Box. But surely, some wrinkle in time coils up and concentrates all its powers for controlling reality in Wyoming bars, where a planned twenty minute stop can easily drift into a five hour adventure, before one even thinks to glance at the clock.

We resisted the black hole of the phone book conversation because we wanted to get checked into our lodging. Gently, we brought the little group at the Invasion out of its ruminations, ordered a beer, and asked for directions to our RV Park. Amanda loaned us the cordless phone and recited from memory the number of the people who owned the two parks in town where it was possible we'd been booked. Our host Christy answered, and told us where to turn to find the correct RV Park, just on the edge of town. We finished our beer and regretfully pulled ourselves away, leaving our bar buddies to their ruminations over the phone book.

In about two minutes we'd driven up Nolan Avenue, past the site of our other planned stop, the Hole in the Wall, and made it to the RV Park. The "cabin" we thought we'd reserved turned out to be a spacious two-bedroom mobile home with a full kitchen and a washer/dryer. At this time of year we had the park nearly to ourselves, save for Christy and her husband Randy, their children, and their bulldog Molly, who enjoyed chasing Spike around in circles before driving him into the mud of a drained stock-pond.

After we got settled in, we had a nice chat with Randy, who was perched on top one of the park's tidy cabins, outfitting it with a new metal roof. As he worked, we told him about the bar tour and he told us about some other interesting spots to visit. He gave us directions to Outlaw Canyon, which would take us to the Hole in the Wall site, where Butch and Sundance had been part of a large, loose group of outlaws known as the Hole in the Wall Gang.

The next day we followed Randy's directions that took us through Willow Creek Ranch, which was in operation in Cassidy's day and is still a working cattle ranch with accommodations for guests. Nineteenth century outlaws might not have been the sharpest tools in the box but they weren't idiots: the hideout is at the end of a long road into the canyon, which put them more than a day's ride from the law. We sailed past meadows greening in early spring and saw livestock and wildlife sharing the bounty of the weather. We navigated the vaguely marked roads and kept in mind Randy's warning lobbed to us from the cabin roof: "The worst mistake you can make is to turn right." As we neared the canyon we were met with a sight that might make a hardened outlaw scoff, and maybe still does. The road into the canyon was blocked by a locked metal gate, with a sign announcing the area would be off limits to vehicle travel for another two weeks. Wildlife is accustomed to spending long cold winters in the shelter of the canyon, and the land managers do their best to keep people away during that especially stressful time.

We parked the car and walked a bit down the road, though the actual Hole in the Wall site was a good ways in and Spike wasn't up for a long hike. We picked up a shiny hubcap we found laying along the road—jetsam from a vehicle that had visited before the road was closed off—and brought it back to the car. Exploration of Outlaw Canyon would have to wait for another visit

We got back to town and entered the Hole in the Wall Bar just in time to join a young man in a toast celebrating his twenty-first birthday. We fell in with the party and told folks we were on a bar tour of Wyoming. Bev, the bartender, made us feel right at home by ribbing us about our residence in the university town of Laramie, which many in Wyoming seem to feel is so pointy-headed intellectual hippie granola tree-huggerish it fits in better with our neighbor to the south. "Laramie?" she asked, straight-faced. "Isn't that in northern Colorado?"

We'd never seen the pre-flood Hole but this new space was more gas-station-retro-urban-funky than any other Wyoming bar we've seen. Lots of things from the old bar didn't survive the flood, but Bev was getting creative in giving the place a new look. Bev has a good eye for design, which shows in the way she's decorated the bar, as well as the gold jewelry she designs and wears in abundance.

She's also quite a collector of local mementoes, including material on a few local heroes whose lives she'd like to celebrate in the bar. Already hanging is a display devoted to Deke Latham, a saddle bronc rider who was ranked fifth in the 1986 PRCA World standings when he died in a car accident not far from Kaycee, where he lived. He was only twenty-one years old. People in Kaycee still celebrate his memory with an annual rodeo.

When we visited, Bev was designing a display commemorating Chris LeDoux, the 1976 PRCA World bareback riding champion and popular country music recording artist, who ranched at Kaycee. He died of liver cancer in 2005, at age fifty-six. Bev has a drawer full of newspaper clippings, photos, and other items related to LeDoux's career, which was given a big boost when Garth Brooks mentioned him in the song *Much Too Young to Feel This Damn Old*. Bev says she could fill the wall with items about his rodeo career, his music career, or both but is going a different way. "He said he wanted to be remembered most as a family man, so that's what I want to put on the wall," she explained.

We spent the weekend in Kaycee meandering from the Invasion to the Hole in the Wall to the restaurant to the RV Park to the area of Outlaw Canyon, drifting like an unanchored canoe in a lake. At our last stop in the Invasion, we chatted a bit more with Amanda, who was intrigued by the Antarctica logo on Ron's hat. We have a friend who'd spent several months working support at a research station there and brought the hat for us as a souvenir. Seeing it prompted Amanda to tell us about some time she spent in New Zealand.

In the background during this conversation, a television suspended above the bar broadcast a cattle auction, and most of the several regulars from our earlier stop were there watching, entranced. As fuzzy brown cattle wandered and chewed, showing their best sides to the television camera, we took a few pictures of the bar and bought a souvenir. It was a baseball cap that said "Invasion Bar" with the "I" formed by a stylized cowboy boot.

We left the Invasion and spent a few more minutes figuratively anchored at the Hole in the Wall before shoving off for Laramie. Bev, along with another bartender named Sue and a few customers, were watching Clark Gable and Marilyn Monroe in *The Misfits* on their big bar television. We selected a coffee mug from the bar's ample souvenir collection, and Bev tossed in a complimentary condom in a package that said "Hole in the Wall Bar—our customers come first." A slow trickle of customers came through, some at the drive-up window and others through the door. One young man came in confused about whether he'd be allowed to use the restroom. Maybe he'd already had a few when he got there, I'm not sure, but in his defense I, too, had been confused by the sign on the door that said this place was a bar, not a gas station (although the old pumps were still in place, shielded by orange netting) and that if people wanted to use the bathroom they should go to the highway rest area just up the road. It sort of sounded like people weren't supposed to come in at all, but the pounding of the jukebox, at least during evening hours, was enough to dispel that possibility.

Teasing by Bev and Sue and us probably didn't help his immediate situation, but as soon as he was assured the place was in fact a bar with restrooms, he relaxed and settled in for awhile. Bev asked if he was "on the methane" and of course the answer was yes. Drilling for coal bed methane employs so many out of state workers that young men like this one, who turned out to be Steve from Iowa, are everywhere. Passing pre-employment and random "piss tests" for drugs, as Steve called them, is a vital condition of employment and test failure accounts for high employee turnover. So many workers drift through Wyoming and make so much money in the energy industry that some don't need to work more than a week. It can be hard for employers to keep up with the paperwork.

The door indeed opened one more time before we left, and in came a trucker who'd blown a tire on his 18-wheeler and had parked it under the highway overpass near the bar. He'd come into the Hole in the Wall looking for directions to the nearest truck stop where he could get the tire repaired and not risk being ticketed for shedding rubber all over the interstate.

Bev asked plenty of knowledgeable questions about whether the wheel was an inner or an outer and whether the trailer was loaded or empty. Weighing his responses to her numerous questions, she looked him in the eye and concluded, "Basically, you are screwed." This was a Sunday, but that didn't matter because there is no truck stop in Kaycee. In fact, he'd best get back on the highway and continue on the sixty miles south to Casper in spite of his truck's handicap. He shouldn't worry too much about shedding rubber; there's not much chance at all he'd be spotted by a patrolman on this stretch of interstate. We concurred; we've been driving around Wyoming a long time and know that patrolmen aren't plentiful. We didn't add that they have an uncanny way of showing up just at the exact moment you wish they wouldn't.

"What is this," the trucker fumed, "some kind of a ghost town?"

Ghost town indeed. The spirits of Deke Latham and Chris LeDoux hang over the place, along with the spirits of all the men and women who have come through this town, died in this town, or hammered out a living throughout its robust winters and scorching summers. A mighty flood like the one that hit in 2002 might wash away buildings, but it won't wash away the sense of connectedness among Kaycee's people like so much flotsam. The Invasion and the Hole in the Wall will give them someplace to take shelter for a long time to come.

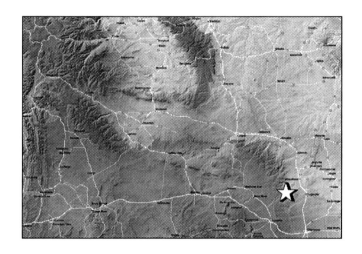

The Long and Winding Road
Shamrock Saloon
Sybille Canyon, Wyoming

Once upon a time, the Shamrock Saloon sat at the eastern approach to Sybille Canyon on Wyoming Highway 34. That winding route shared an ancient channel with North Sybille Creek. Together water and road meandered through the tilted granite layers of the Laramie Range in southeast Wyoming. The Shamrock is still there, but the canyon is gone. Not so much gone, but blasted, widened, straightened, and leveled, making a quicker trip from Wheatland to U.S. 30/287 north of Laramie. The old road once offered a charming visual complement to the Shamrock, whose weather-worn wood façade and front deck look like they could slide off at any moment, like loose rock from a hillside. The new road is race-track smooth, and its drivers might fancy themselves future NASCAR champions as they rocket down the improved 5.4 mile section. No one would dispute that with all that rock out of the way passing is safer, and the multitudes of mule deer that cross the road to water in the creek can be spotted from farther away than before and avoided. But for the casual tourist like me, the winding road with a surprise around every corner was a main reason for the drive.

I've been driving that road occasionally since even before I moved to Wyoming, which was in 1992. The first time I saw the Shamrock my now ex-husband and I were moseying along Wyoming 34 on a warm summer day in the late 1980s, and encountered a long line of orange construction cones down the center of the highway, but no workers or travel delays. No cars to speak of, either. We didn't know the Shamrock existed, so a bar with an Irish name and a big green shamrock sprouting in a lonely canyon offered a temptation we couldn't resist.

We entered the bar, cool and dark with its richly aged wooden walls and sooty windows. Little green shamrocks welcomed us from banners strung around the room. The fireplace with its hearth of smooth round stone was unlit on that summer day, but looked reliable for warming any cool night, summer or winter.

As we visited with the bartender, a man who'd obviously spent his afternoon sheltered in the cool darkness wobbled up to us. He hadn't shaved for awhile, and appeared to be living somewhere without benefit of a washer/dryer.

Focusing on my husband he asked, "Did you see those orange construction cones out on the highway?

"Yeah sure, we saw a long line of them just east of here."

"Oh, good, they're still where I set 'em up. Just checking."

The lone road construction worker then teetered back to his table near the cold fireplace and took another pull on his drink. Good to know road construction was not going to interfere with travel on Wyoming 34 that day. Later on that same Wyoming trip we'd met with construction in another area where there actually was work going on. Instead of the usual lines of traffic being led through the construction area by pilot cars, this was more of a do-it-yourself maneuver. Drivers of the first car in line, we were handed a "Follow Me" flag, instructed to lead traffic and give the flag to the orange-vested worker at the other end of the single-lane, pot-holed, surface-scraped highway. It was a harrowing trip along the remains of the roadway, steep mountain shooting up on one side, death-defying drop-off on the other. But as flag bearers, we couldn't waver, so we steadfastly led the parade.

The Wyoming Department of Transportation wasn't messing around when it tackled the recent round of road work along Wyoming 34. So much rock had to be moved out of the way to straighten and widen the highway through the canyon that a twenty-five-minute drive could take hours. On days when they used dynamite, travelers might as well stay home rather than be parked while seven million-year-old granite was transformed yet again.

All this dynamite blasting created a need for the Wyoming State Archaeologist to be on hand to monitor a sensitive archaeological spot in the canyon known as the

China Wall site. Brian Waitkus from the Office of the Wyoming State Archaeologist, Survey Section, tested and excavated this location from 1996-1999, then a few years later monitored the highway construction near the site.

According to his report, "The Prehistoric site consists of a series of short term campsites ranging in age from 10,650 year ago to five hundred years ago.... The short term camps likely lasted a few days to a couple of weeks in duration. During this time, the small groups of people replaced their worn out or broken stone tools with locally available stone." The report describes how the people hunted big and small game and birds and how they used the various plants that grew there in summer. There was also plenty of water in the form of an exposed spring, so people could spend time there relaxing and recharging their hunter-gathering batteries before moving on.

I like to imagine that people live many lives, and that in a previous one, I was among such a group resting at the China Wall site. I like to picture our little group idling away a few moments skipping rocks across the pristine water while the sun sets on another nomadic day. I can almost recall being in charge of finding the camping spot that afforded the best afternoon shade and early morning warming sun. I bet I found some hollow logs and palm-sized rocks and led the group in percussive after-dinner songs. In spite of the fact that I now cling to Wyoming like a barnacle on a ship's keel, part of me was a full-time nomad in a past life.

I can blame my late Uncle Jay, who passed on about thirty-five years ago. Uncle Jay was my mother's brother. He was born Claude Francis Brennan, Jr. My older brother Doug remembers him better than I: he recalls an introspective, talented, dapper man who was a successful record company executive, until his death at around age sixty. As a boy growing up in St. Louis, Uncle Jay was fascinated by the Mississippi River, which was more aesthetically appealing then than it is today. He was seized by a young man's urge for adventure and exploration so took to the waters of Old Man River and paddled his canoe, solo, toward New Orleans. Uncle Jay may have wished he'd had a companion about the time a snake bit him and he had to make a little slit in his skin with a knife and suck out the venom. The whole story is officially family lore now, though both my mother and her sister are somewhat hazy about their big brother's adventure, and the facts shift with each retelling. But it isn't really the specifics that I find compelling about the trip. It is just that he made it happen.

Recently, Ron and I made our own comparatively tame journey beyond the Mississippi to visit family "back east," as we say in Wyoming. For us that means going to my family in Kansas City and then east to various spots in Indiana, to see parents, siblings, siblings' children, and siblings' childrens' children. Whenever we make that trip I hear the Sirens harmonizing *Ju-lee-aa-anne* as we cross one of the bridges spanning the big river. Lest I go uncontrollably airborne off the bridge deck into the muddy water below, I always have to stop the car and go for a walk along the bank, at least long enough to smell the river breezes. The urge to climb aboard a vessel and float along just to see where I'd wind up pulls me with a force almost too strong to resist it.

So, why do I resist it?

I don't mind the catfish corpses or the unidentifiable objects floating by, but I'm not wild about poison ivy, heat, or humidity, yet I tell myself if I had a spot on the banks of the river, none of those ills would matter. I calculate where I could find a good spot to build a hut just above where the Missouri flows into the Mississippi. Ron, Spike, our cat, our turtle and I could live the hermit's life among the deciduous forest, listening to the tree frogs drone and the seagulls shriek, skipping rocks from the shore. But then I remember the wide open basins and ranges of Wyoming. I remember my past life as a hunter-gatherer and before that, as a high plains antelope. I re-grip the wheel and propel myself down the road, not down the river, at least for now.

Of course, we have rivers in the West: fast, cold, rocky, narrow conduits for glacial water in a rush to reach level land. I love the sound they produce: hydraulic energy bouncing over boulders like high-hat cymbals shaken in a tin can. Maybe I read too much Mark Twain as a kid, or heard too many stories of my Uncle Jay's solo paddling feat. The slow low pulse of big water moving inevitably onward through this last drainage before the water joins the ocean feels the same as the pulse of my own heart and blood moving toward an unknown eternity. But for now, my blood isn't flowing into the wider ocean: it is staying put in my body. The Wyoming bar tour is my Mississippi River, taking me to new surprises at each turn. On this stretch of my life's journey, Sybille Canyon is my navigable channel and the Shamrock my favorite port.

Once, long ago, I stopped at the Shamrock with Ron before we had the idea for a bar tour. The gentleman tending bar had fixed a crock pot full of red chili, in spite of the warm day, and served it to us in big bowls along with saltines and cold beer. We chatted awhile and asked him about the unusual design of a wall clock in the bar. The numbers on the dial were made from rattlesnake rattles. He'd collected them from snakes he'd killed outside, near the bar, across from the elementary school that serves the ranch children of the Canyon.

The chili-cooking man is long gone from the Shamrock. For several years the place has been owned by an industrious woman named Laura. I know her name because she gave me a pen from the bar that says "Stolen from the Shamrock Bar cuz Laura was too cheap to give me one!"

Ron and I typically stop in for short visits as we migrate through the canyon from basin to range or range to basin. Every time we stop, Laura is behind the bar, serving drinks or washing glasses or hanging up another string of whimsical party lights.

At certain times of the year the Shamrock's hours are limited to evenings or weekends. The nearest town is twenty miles away, so most of Laura's customers are the local ranching folks who live and work in the canyon. The important word here is work: they don't take time off in the day to goof off and play pool in a bar, like we do. Instead, they are calving or cutting hay or fixing fence or poring over the accounts or doctoring horses or one of the other endless chores of ranch life.

But in summer the bar is open every day from one to nine p.m. On Friday they stay open "until the cows come home." Sometimes they have music jam sessions, and folks gather to play old time music on guitars, fiddles, mandolins, and whatever else they have on hand. I want to make one of those jams someday, but know I'll embarrass myself by not knowing enough real music by Doc Watson or Bill Monroe or Patsy Cline and others from the Mesopotamia of American music. The best I can do is Elvis.

When I picture the Shamrock, I fancy I can see one of my former selves perched at the bar. It's the self I was when I first set foot in the place in the late 1980s. Through the haze of cigarette smoke and memory I can make out a fair-haired thirty year old in cowboy boots, Wranglers, and a T-shirt with a large image of Elvis's face smiling above the words "I'm Dead" in bright pink letters three inches high. That young woman is smiling with awe at what a life in Wyoming could mean, undaunted by the efforts it would take to achieve. Ah, youth.

The Wyoming dream I had then has been fulfilled but there have been some nightmarish bumps along the road. Happily, believing in past lives means believing in future lives. I'm compelled to always move forward at a steady pace, down the river, up the road, around the bend, to see what is next. I'll cycle back around again, maybe to operate a marina on a river bank in Iowa, overlooking the Mississippi. Maybe Uncle Jay will stop in to rent a boat and talk about music and tides. Maybe I'll come back to run a bar at some wide spot in the road in Wyoming and reconnect with my nomadic clan. In any case, I'll live happily ever after, and ever after.

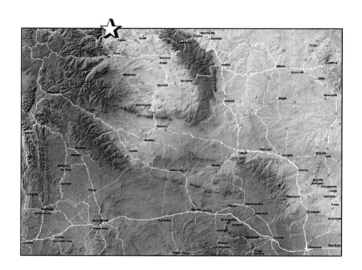

Meditations on Alcohol
Edelweiss Bar
Clark, Wyoming

The Edelweiss Bar in Clark sounds like it should be a chalet in the Swiss Alps, with entertainment provided by the Von Trapp family. With a steady application of imagination, it could be that. The Edelweiss is a ranch-style building made slightly Swiss with the addition of an A-frame porch. Perched along the edge of a mountain stream, its walls festooned with depictions of its namesake little white flower, the bar's setting makes one think of both the Alps and the glorious Rocky Mountains. Julie Andrews as a singing governess wouldn't be out of place in Wyoming's *Sound of Music* setting. Whether or not she would have gone to work as a barmaid is another question.

The Edelweiss sits not in the town of Clark itself but on Wyoming Highway 120, a welcoming outpost on the small town's eastern fringe. That road connects Clark to the town of Cody to the south and Montana to the north. Clark's elevation is low by Wyoming standards, just over four thousand feet, so the mountains that tower over it really do *tower*. Just to the west of town is the Shoshone National Forest. To the west of that is Yellowstone National Park. Surrounding landmarks have names like Dead Indian Summit, Sunlight Basin, and Beartooth Pass, with its summit of over ten thousand feet.

In the late 1920s and early 1930s this still undiscovered area attracted Ernest Hemingway to its extravagant beauty and bountiful hunting and fishing. Hemingway would bump along two-track dirt roads in his Model T, when he wasn't palling around on horseback with ranch hands and fellow writers. Hemingway was as klutzy as he was gifted, unfortunately, and broke more than one bone in this area of Wyoming. He had a serious auto accident after a night camping in Yellowstone. He was driving along the road at dusk and was blinded by the headlights of an oncoming car. As a result, he rolled his car and needed surgery to repair the damage to his body. He wound up spending several months in a Billings, Montana hospital, unable to work on his novel in progress, *Death in the Afternoon*, which as was his custom, he wrote out by hand.

I'm not sure if Hemingway had been drinking when he rolled his car. He was known to enjoy a good bottle of wine for breakfast, and stronger spirits as the day went on. If alcohol was a factor in the accident, Hemingway might have been the first of Wyoming's early drivers to bend a fender under the influence. But he certainly wouldn't have been the last. In fact, Wyoming has some pretty sobering drunk driving statistics and the number of times alcohol has led to highway fatalities makes one wonder why drinking and driving continues to exist in the Wyoming culture. There was once a time when Wyoming roads were lightly traveled and not built for speed. Driving empty roads slowly was not terribly dangerous, and a drink or two passed the time. Just like Indians measured time between destinations by how many sleeps it took to get there (witness Ten Sleep, Wyoming), many modern Wyomingites measure distance by how many beers one could consume while getting there (Sheridan is a six-pack away from Cheyenne).

Today, roads are more crowded and drivers travel at high speeds. Ideally, people wait to drink until they reach their destinations. But according to statistics compiled and published by the state, Wyoming reported a high of 118 alcohol related fatalities in 1982, the first year of reporting. The lowest number of traffic fatalities related to alcohol was in 1997, with forty-four reported. The highest percentage of traffic fatalities that were alcohol related occurred in 1990, with sixty-two percent, and dropped to a low of thirty-two percent in 2000.

The reduced numbers might be due to Wyoming's efforts to correct the problem and change the culture. A few years ago the legislature passed a law against having open containers in a vehicle, at least in the hands of the driver. For passengers it was still okay, but each year the legislature moved toward closing that obvious loophole.

Finally in 2007 a law was passed to stop driving drinkers from simply handing their beverages over to passengers, if stopped by a patrolman.

These sobering statistics were not in my mind when we made our way to the Edelweiss one summer afternoon. A high country fog hung over the mountain foothills occasionally spitting moisture onto our windshield as we drove north through Cody. Once we passed the two main highways leading to the east and northeast entrances of Yellowstone, we virtually had the highway to ourselves. The paved areas of Yellowstone are some of the most tourist-glutted spots on earth during summer, yet it is easy to be alone at its edges.

The Edelweiss in the afternoon offers almost perfect solitude. After our eyes adjusted from the mountain-fog glare of outside to the beer-light lit interior of the Edelweiss, we had our choice of stools and a nice long chat with the bartender. She'd worked there about six months. She'd returned to Wyoming for a job in Riverton after a stint in Yuma, Arizona. Unfortunately, by the time she got back, the job was taken by somebody else. She found the Edelweiss instead, and commutes there each day from Cody. She loved hearing about our bar tour because she'd been on many, herself. She told us that when the time comes she wants her ashes to be scattered along a route from all the bars between Yuma and Butte, Montana.

While we were chatting, the bartender took care of a few other customers who'd stopped to buy gas or pick up a few groceries at this combination bar and convenience stop. I was having my first ever taste of *Jägermeister*, a German liqueur that had always attracted me because of the red deer on the label of the square green bottle.

Jägermeister is a seventy-proof spirit imported from Germany. "Made from a secret recipe of fifty-six herbs and spices, *Jägermeister's* unique taste sets it apart from all other spirits" explains its web site. (Unique is a good way to describe the blend of Luden's cough syrup and grain alcohol flavors, served ice cold.) I'd always wanted to try it, and the Edelweiss seemed a good setting for the adventure. While I was sipping, an outdoorsy-looking couple in their twenties came into the bar, and I thought we'd have some other folks to add to our conversation. Instead, the young man asked the bartender if they could get two "Cap and Sevens" for the road. I was thinking, yeesh, kids, you can't get mixed drinks to go, but of course, this was before the 2007 drinking and driving law went into effect. Before my eyes, the bartender pulled out two twelve ounce Styrofoam cups and mixed the Captain Morgan rum with ginger ale, apologizing that the bar was out of Seven-Up. On went the to-go lids, and out they went, whooshing up the highway toward the national forest, in the shadow of Ernest Hemingway.

One certainly couldn't order a mixed drink to go and drive off, if one was in a Wyoming municipality. But we weren't. Just another example of Wyoming freedoms that treat people like grown ups, but unfortunately potentially put others in danger. Especially these days, as Wyoming attracts ever growing numbers of tourist and out of state energy boom workers. Now we have more than half a million people cluttering up our 97,000 square miles.

My ambivalence about traffic laws and my supreme enjoyment of drinking a seventy-proof liqueur in the middle of the day made me reflect on my own use of alcohol. Could it be that I was sliding into alcohol abuse under the guise of book research? True, Ron and I were careful to limit our drinking and to be sure we had some food before leaving the bar and hitting the road. We almost always just went to one bar per day. But what is a writer if not a seeker of truth? So, I decided to take a closer look at my alcohol habits. I found an online self-assessment quiz connected with the University of Wyoming. I took the test, and here are my results.

1) How often do you have a drink containing alcohol? Never, Monthly or less; 2 to 4 times a month; 2 to 3 times a week; four or more times a week. (That's as high as the ranking goes.)

I was shocked to see that my number of drinks per week, seven, was not only not just toward the top of the scale, it was off the charts. I know there are people who don't drink every day of the week. My own parents would probably have selected the "never" had they been taking the quiz, and the other members of my family would probably be in the monthly or less or two to four times a month category. On the other hand, I've been related by marriage twice to families whose members would be higher up the chart than me, if there were more than seven days in a week. Ron's family is my third set of in-laws, and they aren't frequent drinkers. The same can't be said of my former families-in-law.

My first ex-husband's parents were most certainly alcoholic, and my first ex-husband was, too, although at the time I thought alcoholics were old men without any teeth, passed out in gutters. When we married I was nineteen, he twenty-one. I soon found myself the youngest member of an Al-Anon group in the town where I was attending college when we married. I saw my life: sixty years attending meetings in church basements while my husband attended the AA group next door, smoking and drinking coffee.

That would have been doable had the drinking stopped. Instead, he'd manage to get through about a week at a time before taking the car and driving to Kansas City, about a hundred miles away. He'd see his old friends, stay out all night, and come home the next day hung over, thanks to having drained our bank account through the ATM machine. When hospitalization and therapy didn't work for my first ex-husband, it was time for me to leave.

2) How many drinks containing alcohol do you have on a typical day when you are drinking? Chose 1-12, then 13-24, 25-48; then greater than 48.

I indicated two: now I feel a little better. I might drink as predictably as the setting of the sun or the motion of the tides, but the quantity is apparently on the low side. I'm only on the second question of this quiz, but I'm feeling a bit paranoid and defensive already. Is that a sign of alcoholism? So I drink a couple glasses of wine with dinner nearly every night. In the summer I might precede that with a can of beer and a handful of peanuts, consumed out on the deck while watching goldfinches cover the thistle feeder. Cocktail hour and wine with dinner: only civilized, right? Heck, in France they give little kids wine for breakfast, right?

3) Thinking about a typical week, on how many days do you have at least one alcoholic drink? (If you don't drink every week, answer for a typical week in which you do)

I answered this question the same way I answered the first one: seven. Are they trying to trip me up?

4) How often do you have six or more drinks on one occasion?
Choose between: Never, less than monthly; monthly, weekly, daily or almost daily

Geez Louise, never! Not since high school, anyway. My friend Suzy and I used to go to a 21-club across the state line, while we were still in high school and even underage for the 18-bars in our own state. With fake IDs and some extra makeup, it was easy for us to get in. We didn't go there for the drinks: we went there to hear the great live bands and to dance with cute guys. During several hours of dancing in a hot crowded nightclub, six cheap beers on tap would have gone down easy. Now that

I'm older and my metabolism has changed, beer no longer evaporates through sweat, but instantly converts to pee. I'm over it.

5) Thinking about the past year, what is the greatest number of drinks you've had on any one occasion? Choose one: 1 through 9 or more

I'm glad to see they've narrowed down the time frame so I don't have to factor in those miscreant early years. I picked "four." I was not a regular drinker even after I became legal and went to college. I drank a beer or two on social occasions, but I didn't usually have a drink with meals. Even ex-husband number one didn't keep beer in the refrigerator very often. He'd just buy it when he was ready to drink it all in one sitting. I recall once coming home from an eight hour shift washing dishes in the hospital kitchen where I worked to put myself through college. In my absence he'd decided we needed a brick fireplace in the backyard of our small home.

He had no masonry experience, but that didn't matter. The only thing he needed was a couple six-packs of Coors Tallboys. I came home that evening to a mess of concrete and brick in the backyard, and a morosely soggy husband, crying over his failure. Being married to ex-husband number one stifled my appetite for alcohol. These days the four drinks I indicated in my answer would be consumed very slowly, at the pace of one per hour. If it is only one drink an hour, I'm not sure that even count as "one occasion."

6) How often during the last year have you found that you were not able to stop drinking once you had started? Chose one: Never, less than monthly; monthly, weekly, daily or almost daily.

I thank the Lord God above that my answer is Never. Even in my younger days, alcohol would make me sleepy, and I'd be snoozing after just a couple, unless I was up and about dancing. Maybe I should factor in the fact that I do drink daily. Does not stopping mean from one day to the next, not just lots of drinks in a row? I'm not sure. I guess I could skip a day here and there. In fact, after I had surgery a few years ago and was on pain pills, I had no problem having pasta without *chianti*, or salmon sans *pinot grigio*. But the thought of a glass of ice water with dinner shoots me back into memories of the rather Spartan culinary customs of my parents.

7) How often during the last year have you failed to do what was normally expected from you because of drinking? Chose one: Never, less than monthly; monthly, weekly, daily or almost daily.

I suppose I fail to do what is expected of me as often as any other person, but I attribute that failing to the human condition, not to alcohol. Life with ex-husband number one was hellish, but at least it taught me how awful things can really be, and what a real alcohol problem looks like. After I'd been married just over a month, my father died suddenly, just a few months after he'd retired. He had been an energetic man, though, and decided to take up real estate sales as a second career. Dad was driving his car when he felt a bit dizzy, so he pulled into the local gasoline station where the mechanic called an ambulance for him. He was admitted into a hospital. Instead of being released the next morning as planned, he died there, instead.

Ex-husband number one had his good qualities, and he was very kind and supportive of my family the first few days of our grief. He was at my side for the Catholic wake at the funeral home, entering in conversations with relatives and my father's business associates. He was there through the long funeral mass and the burial on a slate grey February day. But after several hours of making conversation with strangers and watching people cry, he needed some time away. We stayed at his parent's house during the funeral events. The night after the funeral I went to bed early, and he went out with friends. At about three a.m. the phone rang, and his father answered. Ex-husband number one had gotten pulled over, ticketed with a DUI, and thrown in jail. My father-in-law went to bail him out and bring him home. So no, compared to that, I've never not done what was expected of me because of drinking.

8) How often during the last year have you needed a first drink in the morning to get yourself going after a heavy drinking session? Chose one: Never, less than monthly; monthly, weekly, daily or almost

Never, although I hear it helps, and I've been tempted a few times when I've awakened with a hangover. It just seems so icky and depraved I've never tried the hair of the dog.

9) How often during the last year have you had a feeling of guilt or remorse after drinking? Chose one: Never, less than monthly; monthly, weekly, daily or almost daily.

I'm a recovering Catholic, so guilt and remorse are still the lenses through which I assess my performance in life. Catholics need to be bad in order to enlist the aid of someone to pray for them, to intercede for them, with God. That's when saints spring into action. There's a patron saint of brewers named St. Arnold. He was born in Austria in 580, and became a priest and eventually a bishop before his death in 640. He'd long espoused the virtues of beer and of its brewers, especially in light of the health dangers of drinking the water in those times. After his burial in France, his hometown wanted his body returned to Austria, so it was exhumed and the long, hot journey began. When the pallbearers reached an inn where they'd hoped to quench their thirst, they were told there was only enough beer to fill one mug, and they'd have to share. But lo! There was plenty to go around, and everyone's thirst was satisfied. Turning water into beer was St. Arnold's miracle. So, do I ever feel guilty because of drinking? No. But if I did, I'd know where to turn for help.

10) How often during the last year have you been unable to remember what happened the night before because you had been drinking? Chose one: Never, less than monthly; monthly, weekly, daily or almost

I chose never. I may forget things sometimes, but I think that is a sign of aging and overwork, not alcohol abuse.

11) Have you or someone else been injured as a result of your drinking? Chose one: Never, Yes, but not in the last year; Yes, in the last

No. I don't operate motor vehicles or sharp knives, or write books, without extreme caution.

12) Has a relative or friend or a doctor or other health worker been concerned about your drinking or suggested you cut down? Chose one: No, Yes, but not in the last year; Yes, in the last year.

No. However, that might be because I rarely go to the doctor. I whisk my pets off to the vet at the first sign of a sneeze, but I troupe along and overcome or ignore whatever my body might dish out. Besides, I drink plenty of red wine, enough to wash away the *brie* and *baguettes* that might otherwise deposit fat in arteries.

After answering a few demographic questions I'd completed the Alcohol Awareness survey. I clicked Submit and in the time it takes to pop a champagne cork I got my results.

Here they are:

Based on Your Responses: Your results on the AUDIT (Alcohol Use Disorders Identification Test) are below the range usually associated with harmful drinking or alcoholism. However, you may be at increased risk for health problems due to the number of alcoholic drinks you reported consuming per week, and from how much you have consumed on at least one occasion. For women and anyone over sixty-five, having more than seven drinks a week increases the risk for negative health consequences. In addition, consuming too much alcohol on one occasion increases your risk for injury and other immediate consequences. This risk is associated with having more than three drinks per occasion if you are a woman or someone over sixty-five.

Many people are not aware of how their alcohol consumption compares to that of the general public. More than 96.5% of the general adult American population, and 99% of women, consume fewer drinks per week than you reported consuming.

Recommended action: Because your results indicate that your alcohol consumption many be increasing your risk for health problems, consider cutting back the amount of alcohol you drink to safer levels. For some people, especially for those with an early or undetected alcohol problem, quitting may be the best choice. And in some situations no amount of alcohol is safe.

Good advice, perhaps. But I have a tough time believing the statistics that say only one percent of American women have more drinks a day than I do. Is that a percentage of test takers, or really of all women? I'd also like to have some broader health context. For example, I bet I eat far less junk food and drink far less soda pop than the average American woman or man. I wear my seatbelts, look both ways before crossing the street, and take the stairs instead of the elevator to my fourth floor office. I try to fill my head with positive thoughts, and my life with positive people. I love my husband and my family, and they love me. Could I be a better person? Heck, yes. Could I be a healthier person? No doubt. I prefer not to live obsessed with life's tiny ingredients: pinches of recklessness and dashes of idiocy won't ruin the balance of what is shaping up to be a wonderful experience on the earth. Life should be about adding things: creating what Hemingway called a "moveable feast." Maybe old Papa Hemingway isn't such a bad model, after all.

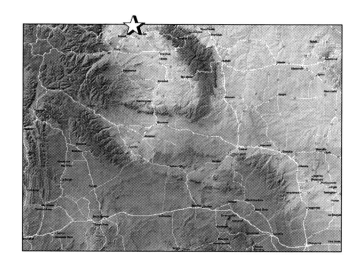

The Longest Running Show on Earth
Frannie Bar
Frannie, Wyoming

The Frannie Bar is precisely named, since it is the only bar in Frannie, a town of two hundred residents in the northern tip of the Big Horn Basin. The building resembles an Old West jail where Gary Cooper might have spent an unquiet night on the porch, defending an incarcerated cattle rustler from an impromptu necktie party at the local hanging tree. In the building's false Western façade, a pair of swinging saloon doors painted in silhouette black adorn the white front door. In each silhouette a white cutout of a liquor bottle leaves no doubt that this is a bar—not a restaurant or microbrewery—a *bar*.

It isn't the sort of place where travelers commonly pop in. None of the familiar trappings of the tourist trade are visible, as they are when one draws closer to Cody and Yellowstone Park to the west. No signs for ATM machines and bus parking; no chainsaw-carved bears on the porch; no promise of free lunches for the kiddies. Entering the bar as a stranger takes either a powerful thirst or a powerful curiosity about what's behind the door. We had both, so we shook off the uncomfortable feeling of walking uninvited into a stranger's living room in the middle of the afternoon and pushed open the front door into the smokiest bar we'd ever been in.

Even though only four people were inside, they each seemed to be smoking at least one cigarette at a time, and none went for more than a few minutes between nicotine fixes. But when trying to fit in as an outsider in an insiders' bar, the wrong thing to say is "Damn, it's smoky in here. Open a window." So we asked our lungs for forgiveness and made our way to some stools beneath the SmokeEater, which had long ago gasped its last.

Through the haze we made out a rectangular room with a long bar, a dart machine, and some tall tables and chairs. Jackalopes, bar lights and bumper stickers dotted the cedar paneled walls. At the back of the backroom, past the pool table, the restroom hunkered. On two sides of the main room, windows dimly revealed the parking lot and street. The bartenders could look out the drive-thru window from their vantage point behind the bar and see customers approach. "Here comes Bill," one might say. Then they'd pop open a can of Bill's favorite brew and have it waiting on a coaster in front his regular stool before the foam could bubble from the opening. One can almost hear the theme song from *Cheers* playing *Where Everybody Knows Your Name*. It's that kind of place.

The bartenders and owners of the Frannie Bar are named Ron and Melanie. He has a job in a limestone quarry just up the road in Montana; she has been an oilfield roughneck, a farmer, and a teacher of PE and art. She "loved the camaraderie" of those jobs, and has at least as much of it at her fulltime gig at the Frannie Bar. She tells us that Frannie got its motto, the "biggest little town in Wyoming," because the town straddles the county line between Big Horn and Park counties. Montana is two miles up U.S. 310. So it's logical that the bar's t-shirts read "Frannie Bar. Takes up two counties and damn near two states."

Frannie the town was named for then six-year-old Frannie Morris, daughter of Mr. and Mrs. Jack Morris. In the late 1880s, Mr. Morris opened a post office on his ranch on Sage Creek, and named the post office/town after his daughter. He sometimes entertained guests such as Buffalo Bill Cody at the ranch.

Frannie later spent time performing with Buffalo Bill's *Wild West Show*. A cloisonné image of the young Frannie in a long skirt astride a bucking bronc graces an official town pin. Frannie may have been a trick rider in the show, or a sharp shooter like the famous Annie Oakley; those records are lost.

Whatever her specialty, she was one of many performers in a Western spectacle created by Buffalo Bill, one of America's most accomplished promoters and showmen. He was a soldier, buffalo hunter, and actor, by turns. He knew something about taking humdrum aspects of workaday Western life, such as shooting firearms and herding livestock, and turning them into a thousand thrills designed to captivate audiences in America and Europe. The show started in the 1880s and continued until the start of the First World War. Cody was as responsible as anyone for creating the Western myths of the heroic cowboy and dangerous Indian, and the grand calling of a life on horseback.

Cody faced the problem that gnaws at all storytellers like fleas in a blanket: how to take ordinary life and give it drama, make it artistic entertainment, filled with complication and tension and hope. He could have created a formal stage play about the cowboy life and developed a multi-faceted protagonist as leading man. Instead, he hit upon the idea of reenacting glamorous Western motifs and placing himself in the center of the ring. He was the heroic figure taming savages, ridding the plains of the pesky buffalo, making the West safe for schoolmarms and urchins. Even in the early twentieth century when most Indians resided on reservations, and cattle and barbed wire and railroad tracks replaced bison and open range and winter camps, Cody presented the West according to his own sense of glory and conquest. And people bought what he was selling.

The modern West, too, offers its stock characters and easy themes for today's storytellers. Cowboys, tourists, environmentalists, miners, bartenders, boom time laborers, fourth-generation ranchers and their first generation college student offspring, all living lives against a backdrop of towering mountains or windswept plains—

these form the world of most stories about the historic or contemporary West, including bar tour stories.

Ron and I walk into a bar as strangers and in a couple hours we hope to make acquaintance with bartenders and customers, not as objective researchers might do, but as people with a real interest in the places and people we find. Being both a beer buddy and a student of the bar life has turned out to be awkward in ways I hadn't imagined when I started writing about bars. When I leave my new friends behind after an hour or two of socializing and spending money on T-shirts and beers, I have to decide what to do with the story. I prefer not to trot out the people I meet like so many trick riders and whip crackers, giving them a spin around the arena for my readers, presenting them like specimens of the Rural West. I like to think my stories are authentic, and not exploitive of people's circumstances. But just like Cody, the stories I tell are really about me.

My belief is that each bar comprises a close-knit rural community, a place where everyone goes, to drink or not, because there are so few other places to meet. There's a good chance that my belief colors my experiences of my brief trip to each bar. I want to find friends: I make friends. I want to find *Cheers*: I find *Cheer*s. I want to find places that will outlast booms and busts and old timers dying off, so I picture myself stopping back by in another twenty years and finding the place unchanged.

If I have fallen prey to my own nostalgia, most of the blame is on me, but some of it is simply on the nature of bars. There is a certain sameness to each of them, in spite of the diversity of climate and culture that lies just outside each front door. Inside, the same jukebox, the same jackalope, the same pool table and liquor bottles and beer signs and familiar cast of characters on either side of the bar, all invite a sense that time has stopped, the curtain has risen, and the next scene in a stage play without end has begun.

"What will you have, friend?" is a powerful opening line, seductive to anyone with a desire to fit in. Like most writers, I find that desire to belong causes my head to spin, a bit. Writers are natural outsiders, figuratively observing the melee of a dodge ball game from the corner of the playground. Being in the center of the circle changes the game and makes the story difficult if not impossible to tell objectively. Like theories of time travel suggest, it is impossible to enter a moment without forever changing it. Just like the pretty nurse selling poppies from a tray on the Beatles' *Penny Lane*, though I feel as if I'm in a play, I am anyway....

It was hot outside on the afternoon of this particular bar performance, so Ron and Melanie let us bring Spike in from the car where we'd parked in the shade. Spike has a rather conservative personality, bordering on aloof, but is so cute that he instantly attracts gushy attention. He coolly avoided too much petting and made himself busy snuffling up stale popcorn from cracks between the worn linoleum and the edge of the bar. While he went about that rather disgusting business, we talked to Ron and Melanie about some other stops on the bar tour, and noticed a framed cartoon of a naked woman swimming in the ocean, her large behind extruding a stream of water through her "blowhole." The caption read "Save the Whales."

We recognized the artwork from the walls of another stop on the bar tour: Rowdy's Spirits & Bait in Hyattville. Turns out Ron and Melanie are friends of Rowdy and his wife, who'd recently sold the bar and moved down the road to Ten Sleep. Apparently Rowdy dispersed some of his artwork to the Frannie Bar. We were sad to think about one of our favorite Wyoming bar owners being poorly. We clinked beer bottles to his health.

The couple smoking at the far end of the bar, regular Frannie patrons, soon joined the conversation. He is a road construction worker and she runs the household. As we talked we noticed through the drive up window that a regular customer had just pulled up and was headed into the bar. Melanie had his favorite beer breathing on a coaster before the door swung open. He was on his way to his shift as a security guard on an oil rig. He drank his beer, told us a bit about what it is like to guard an oil rig on the night shift ("Usually it's pretty quiet out there") and bought the house a round on his way out. Spike watched hopefully as the door swung open again, wishing in vain it was time to leave and lie down on his comfortable back seat. Apparently the popcorn was all gone.

Pretty soon in came another man, who'd stopped for a beer after having been to a ranch auction. He'd bought a tractor, which he thought would come in handy. He also bought a whole box of homemade wine that had been corked and aged in Lancer's wine bottles. The year on the box was 1982. The label announced the variety as tomato. We debated about whether the wine would "still" be good. In spite of a dulling of the appetite at the thought of tomato wine, we ordered a small pizza to soak up some of the beer before we hit the road again. I went back to the freezer next to the pool table in the back room to hand-select the Red Baron variety, as if it were a fine wine. Spike approved the finished product that Melanie heated for us in the toaster oven.

We asked the assembled company for advice about motels in Lovell, where we were headed. The next day we were planning to explore the wild mustang range in the Pryor Mountains that lay just outside that town, straddling the state line. We were warned away from a few motels with the words "definitely don't go there."

As always, it would have been too easy to stay around and see who would step through the door next and what their stories would be. Perhaps young Frannie herself would pop in and tell us what her specialty was in the Buffalo Bill Wild West Show. We could tell her about our garden back in Laramie, and our bird watching and home improvement projects that fill many of our days. Maybe the regular customers would enjoy hearing these stories from bar-touring strangers as much as we enjoyed theirs. But they already had their own stage, their own actors, and their own season tickets for a regular stool. The show will go on for our new friends without us, and the Frannie Bar will be here for good, just as it is. In twenty years we could go back and visit the same people, and Spike could still find popcorn on the floor. Nothing could change the greatest show on earth.

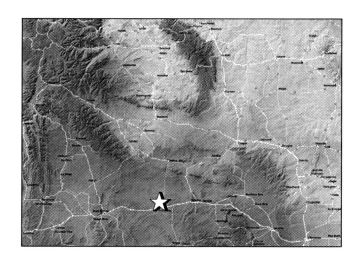

Three Tales of a City
Desert Bar
Wamsutter, Wyoming

The following stories tell the tale of Wamsutter and its Desert Bar. "The Legend of Desert Jim's" was told to me by my friend Colin Keeney. "What about Wamsutter" is the headline of an Associated Press story that appeared in the *Salt Lake Tribune* on June 12, 2005. "Wamsutter Thanksgiving" is about our stop at the Desert Bar, the day after Thanksgiving, 2005.

The Legend of Desert Jim—Part I

The year was 1970. Colin and some of his buddies were working in the mines out around Rock Springs and Green River, in the southwestern part of the state. When they had some time off they'd drive along I-80 to Laramie, about two hundred miles to the east, to shake off the dust and grime of mine work. Driving across the Red Desert in

Sweetwater County can give a miner a powerful thirst. Happily, refreshment came about midway through the journey, in the form of a beer stop at Desert Jim's.

"You could see the tall oil derrick-shaped sign from I-80," Colin recalls. "Hell, you could even see it from Rawlins. It just said BAR. The town then was tiny, not the metropolis it is today."

On this particular night, a perfect storm of working men, and a few women, all had the same idea of converging at Desert Jim's. Oil workers, railroad workers, men from the mines, got thirsty all at once and jockeyed for space on Jim's barstools. The throng that showed up temporarily doubled or even tripled Wamsutter's tiny population.

Desert Jim himself was an old guy who probably once was tall, but like a lot of aging cowboys, too many falls off horses had taken their toll on his posture. Now he stood half his former height because of a stove-up back.

The bar didn't have much size to it, either. Viewed from the dirt parking lot, the narrow Western façade suggested a bar of about twenty feet in width, and about as many in depth. The bar's size was deceptive from the outside. Though the twenty foot width wasn't far from the truth, the depth was probably closer to fifty feet. The space was efficiently divided up into bar, booths, and occasional makeshift stage and dance floor.

On this night, the working men and a few brave women were gamely trying to dance to a one-man band. That industrious musician was singing wheezily along to his own strumming guitar and hooting harmonica and knee thwapping percussion. Everyone was looking for fun in this tiny place, and behind the bar Desert Jim was setting them up.

What About Wamsutter—Part I

"No one bothers to plant trees or flowers in this blight on the harsh Red Desert. Trailer homes line the sad, barren streets—ready to be hitched up and hauled away at any time. Those gravel roads are a stark symbol of impermanence in a boomtown so temporary many of the men who live here left their families back home."

These words appeared in the *Salt Lake Tribune*, in a story by Associated Press reporter Angie Wagner. They present a bleak viewpoint not far from the one I once held of the town, even though I had never been there. I'd only seen it from I-80, off to the south across an expanse of basin land. Driving through the Red Desert, I thought Wamsutter appeared tumbledown and rusted up, a chaotic collection of streets and houses dancing without a band.

Back in the late 1980s when I first began excursions to Wyoming from my home in the less imaginative Midwest, I fell in love with every town and mountain, and all the geography in between. Dubois: Wooden sidewalks and daily "Pony Express" mail delivery system were romantic and fun. Cheyenne: After my first visit to the Frontier Days Rodeo and concurrent parties, I naively wondered if the town was always that wild, if reveling in the streets took place daily or was somehow connected to the rodeo. Yellowstone Lake: Would the grizzly bears come right down the hiking trail and dine upon me and my Chihuahua, Bonnie, as we strolled along the shore?

Somehow Wamsutter was one place I could not get my mind around. What in the world were people doing stubbed like cigarettes out there in the desert? No streams, no towering mountains, no obvious purpose to this collection of crooked streets and lanes. The metal parts of houses and heavy equipment I could not name glittered in the high sun as I sped past on the interstate. If I was on my way home, I wanted to get there too badly to stop. If I was on my way somewhere else, I wasn't going to pull off the highway and drive the short distance to the town itself. What for? There wasn't anything to see. Not even the BAR sign that protruded above the wreckage was going to lure me in.

Wamsutter Thanksgiving—Part I

It was the day after Thanksgiving, 2005. Rather than struggling through the quicksand that is modern day airports to visit family, we stayed in Wyoming but took an out of town trip for a holiday. This was the year we went to Jackson Hole and Bondurant for the holiday. We had a great time in Jackson, hiking around the Tetons, visiting the National Museum of Wildlife Art, chatting up folks at the Silver Dollar Bar. There we met a pair of pilots who were reciting one-liners, like the countdown to takeoff, around the horseshoe-shaped bar. One joked that the other used to be a highway construction flagger, but became an airplane pilot because he needed work that was less stressful.

We left Jackson the day after Thanksgiving and headed back to Laramie. Since starting this bar tour, we upgrade every trip out of town, no matter the reason, into a stop at a watering hole. This time Wamsutter was on the return route, and it was early enough in the day that we could stop, visit for an hour, and still get to Laramie before dark.

We pulled off I-80 and made for the BAR sign that protruded from the center of town. The trick was selecting the correct road that actually would lead us there. The first road dead-ended in a trailer park. The next swooped us unceremoniously around the outskirts of town and flung us back out into the desert. Reconnoitering, we picked and poked our way through streets that seemed to laugh at our attempts at getting there from here. At last! Help came in the form of a non-Wamsutterite who nevertheless knew her way around: a sympathetic Federal Express driver. What she thought about a pair of holiday drivers stuck out on the edge of town asking how to get to the bar, when the sign that said BAR stuck up from the center of town like a grain elevator on the prairie, we'll never know. She gave a few efficient directions which we followed without error, and we found a curving main road leading past the little café, the beauty parlor, and the Desert Inn, which form the heart of Wamsutter.

The Legend of Desert Jim—Part II

The singing and strumming and drinking and dancing were at full throttle when a pickup truck and horse trailer pulled into the parking lot. Colin recalls California plates and lettering on the side of the truck that spelled out something about Palomino Horses. These people, too, had been traveling along I-80 when they felt the magnetic pull of Desert Jim's. Plus, they'd seen the bright lights blaring BAR. So they parked the truck and trailer, told the Palomino they wouldn't be long, and stepped into the ruckus.

The woman of the pair attracted notice primarily by being one of the only women present. Also, she was a good looker and snazzily dressed, with lots of shiny silver and turquoise jewelry. She quickly became the favored dance partner of the steadily more inebriated miners and railroad men. The one-man band wheezed, Desert Jim poured drinks, and everyone jockeyed for a chance to dance with Mrs. Palomino. After this state of affairs had gone on for some time, Mr. Palomino quietly slipped out the door and headed for his truck in the parking lot.

No one knows how much time passed, but suddenly the door to Desert Jim's flew open and in came Mr. Palomino, brandishing a bullwhip "smack smack smack" over the heads of customers in the densely crowded bar. Naturally, in this tiny place, no one was too happy about the display.

Then Desert Jim, smoking a cigar behind the bar, says "I wonder if you can cut this cigar in half with that bullwhip."

The one-man band oofs to a stop. Lots of muttering and whispering from the crowd vibrates the air.

Mr. Palomino says: "Sure, I'm an expert at this. I'm a Marksman."

So Desert Jim thrusts his chin and cigar out over his bowed-in chest to make a good target. *Whack!* goes the bullwhip, whipping Desert Jim around the ribcage.

A howl goes out from Desert Jim, cigar still secured in his teeth.

"Grumble grumble," says the drunkish crowd.

"Wait a minute, that's OK," says Desert Jim to calm the throng. "Try it again, I'm all right."

Mr. Palomino takes another drink and careful aim. *Whack!* This time the whip wraps around Desert Jim's neck and face.

"Ow!" again.

More, even louder grumbling from the group. Desert Jim, unperturbed, and Mr. Palomino, maybe a bit shaken, reach deep inside themselves, determined to take another stab at it. Finally, *Crack! Snap!* Mr. Palomino cuts the cigar clean in two. The crowd cheers, orders another round, congratulates Mr. Palomino, and the one-man band lurches into full voice. Mr. Palomino disappears back outside and is gone for some time. Mrs. Palomino keeps dancing with the boys. No one really wonders about the whereabouts of her husband. A good time is being had by all, and Desert Jim seems unfazed by his injuries.

What About Wamsutter—Part II

My former view of Wamsutter was echoed by the Associated Press reporter, and apparently commonly held by outsiders and Wyomingites alike. Wamsutter, by the early 1980s, was on the lee side of a mighty wind of an energy boom that had fueled lots of tiny Wyoming towns situated near oil and gas reserves. With the loss of a market willing to pay top dollar for those products, workers left towns like Wamsutter to stand nearly empty. According to Wagner, Wamsutter housed close to fifteen hundred people in the boom years, and dwindled to around two hundred after the bust ushered people away. Lots of other towns faced the same fate, including Jeffrey City to the north, where uranium was once mined.

Boom and bust has long been Wyoming's way, like the inhale and exhale of the wind or the dumping and melting of snow. We are used to cycles. Although it makes us nervous and uncomfortable to wait, we know change is always around the corner. Today, enough change has come to the national and international energy market that Wamsutter is once again booming, and most of Wyoming can say the same. Wyoming is one of the few states to be operating with a budget surplus, thanks to the boom.

Thanksgiving in Wamsutter—Part II

The Desert Bar appears tiny from the outside—not very wide, and not very much deeper than before the addition was put onto the back. The outside wall is decorated with desert landscape tableau. Left, a man wearing overalls and a miner's helmet stands holding a beer bottle and gazing into the middle distance. Right, an oil derrick spurts. Center, "Desert Bar Wamsutter Wyo." is hand-lettered.

My notion of Wamsutter as Wyoming's armpit and the Desert Bar as that armpit after a brisk workout was about to evaporate like a puddle on a shower floor. We pushed open the door and saw...a bar, a bunch of barstools, two women bartenders, a couple of male customers, a row of booths, Western folk art on the walls, and beer for sale. No brawling oil patch workers throwing punches, no creepy toothless guys in dark corners offering us methamphetamine. The bartenders nodded us a greeting, asked what we'd like, and served it to us, just like we belonged there. And right away we felt we did.

After we started sipping our first beer, one of the bartenders came down the length of the bar to chat with us. Valeta is a longtime area resident who often works in the bar to help out the owner. She told us there was a ton of food left over from Thanksgiving dinner the day before and that we were welcome to help ourselves. There, in the back of the bar, near the pool table, was a collection of crock pots and electric chafing dishes full of turkey, dressing, green beans, and all the traditional Thanksgiving fixings. Because Wamsutter is usually stuffed with single working men, the gals at the bar thought they'd all need somewhere to go for a holiday dinner. Turns out most of the "boys" took advantage of the time off and went somewhere else, probably back home to their wives and families. So the leftover food was there for the eating, and we helped ourselves to fixings and felt bad we'd ever thought there was nothing special about Wamsutter.

The Legend of Desert Jim—Part III

Then suddenly the door to Desert Jim's bursts open and in rides the bullwhip marksman Mr. Palomino, on a fully saddled golden-coated steed. Well, the crowd wasn't too crazy about sharing a tiny bar with a large equine. But Desert Jim took one look at it, and his eyes got glazed and moist. He glanced out the window of the bar, across the darkening sage-colored desert. In a voice choked with fine sand and cigar smoke, he said, "I haven't been on a horse in years." With that he took over the reins from Mr. Palomino, and rode that horse right out the door.

Since it appeared Desert Jim might be gone for awhile, and the crowd was getting thirsty, Colin and his friends took over as bartenders. No complicated drinks mixed, no change made, just an even swap of a dollar for a beer. They continued on that way through the night, with no more sign of Desert Jim.

Colin found one of his friends, a railroad telegrapher based in Wamsutter, "resting" on the sidewalk as dawn broke the next morning.

"That was the most fun I ever had," the friend managed to say with thickened tongue, as he gazed out into the desert sunrise. As they mused over the highlights of the previous night's bacchanalia, they thought they saw an old cowboy clutching the silken mane of a glistening

Palomino, charging through the bunchgrass and sage, scattering the skittering antelope that got in their way.

What About Wamsutter—Part III

Men stacked nine high in trailers plopped onto newly graded lots scattered along newly bladed roads. Men making forty dollars an hour helping send Wyoming's hidden underground treasures to energy users out of state in return for money, and lots of it. Men, some single, some with families somewhere back home. Families with children whose mothers don't want to live stacked in trailers, with little prospect of jobs or sociability for themselves outside of the bar, café, or church. Women who don't want to pull their children out of their familiar surroundings to attend a thing called Desert School. Sometimes men who make lots of money and don't have much to do with their spare time get into trouble. In rural Wyoming, like much of the rural West, that trouble takes the form of methamphetamine. Sometimes that trouble comes to Wamsutter.

Wyoming is afflicted by meth addiction, and law enforcement can barely keep up with the results. In many places around the state, violent crimes are on the rise, drug addicts struggle to come clean, children live in homes contaminated with ammonia and other drug cooking toxins, and dwellings used as meth labs need extensive remediation before they can be inhabited again.

Another place for remediation may be the Red Desert area of the Great Divide Basin, an environmentally sensitive dwelling place for elk, wild horses, fifty thousand antelope, and many other creatures. Environmentalists are seeking protection for some northern areas of the desert in concert with the Bureau of Land Management and various energy extraction companies who want to figure out how to remove coal bed methane and other products from beneath the ground without totally trashing what lies above it. At the south end of the Red Desert, energy companies plan combined projects around Wamsutter that call for up to 8,950 new natural gas wells, including from one hundred to five hundred coal-bed methane wells, to be drilled over the next thirty to forty years. They also plan to invest in housing and infrastructure in Wamsutter so workers can bring their families and not live stacked up in "man camps," where beds and showers are scheduled based on workers' shifts.

Small towns such as Wamsutter try to cope with significant and usually negative changes they endure to feed the country's vampiric energy needs. Many in Wyoming are proud to be blood contributors. Even those who aren't so proud realize it is a done deal. Angie Wagner talks about the boom-bust cycle and says, "Pessimism hangs over Wamsutter like a blanket of smoke in the town's only bar." She thinks the pessimism is because the town residents know they are headed for another bust and one day the money will cease to flow. She's doesn't realize that the boom itself plunges many of us into depression. At least those whose livelihood doesn't depend on it.

Thanksgiving in Wamsutter—Part III

After our Thanksgiving dinner we spent some more time chatting with bartender Valeta. She told us with pride what a nice town Wamsutter is, how the church and café and beauty parlor give the town a real sense of community. And the school, too. The boys who come to work the oil patch feel homesick some of the time without their families, so they come to the Desert Bar where Valeta and the other women act as their second moms.

We told Valeta we were on a bar tour of Wyoming and asked if we could take some pictures of the place. She said we could, but first made sure we weren't like that newspaper reporter who came and wrote about her town. She thought the story made the town look terrible, nothing like the nice community it really is. We told her we'd seen the story in the Salt Lake newspaper a few months back. As we commiserated, she told us more about the area's amenities and a little bit about life in the Great Divide Basin.

Valeta, who I guessed is in her sixties now, told us about her earlier days in south-central Wyoming in the 1970s. She came out here from Arkansas. Her husband was an oil field worker. They had a trailer house that they plopped out right in the Red Desert along with their children, just to the west of Wamsutter. They had no near neighbors, and no electricity for the trailer. Her mother back in Arkansas could not understand why Valeta would agree to live that way. Valeta's mother had endured enough years without electricity and such, and once she finally got those modern conveniences she would never willingly have given them up.

Eventually, Valeta's husband concocted a plan to power up the trailer with the help of an old Ford Capri. First he removed the guts of the car's interior. Next he put in an electric generator where the seats had been. Then he hooked the generator up to the drive line through a hole in the car floor. He ran a line from the generator to the trailer. He'd turn on the ignition to the car and shazam! Power! Valeta wasn't too crazy about this invention, though. Between the idling of the engine and the running of the generator, it was too noisy in the trailer for her to hear herself think. She hardly ever needed electricity badly enough to endure it.

Valeta served us up another beer to go with our turkey dinner and gave us a book of bar matches. A cartoon cowboy on the flap brandished a pistol and said, "We Aim at Pleasing You and We Hope we Hit the Mark." We helped ourselves to home baked pumpkin cookies, while Valeta told us how her family came to leave the pioneer life in Red Desert. They moved into Wamsutter, motivated in part by the forty-eight mile one way bus ride along I-80 to Rawlins that took the kids to school each day. Any complication of blizzard or white out could put the whole system on the fritz. Now her kids are grown and she seems content living in town. She has a new group of kids to look after: the boys who work the oil fields, who might get into trouble if it weren't for their surrogate mom, and who might just get lonely enough to hot wire a water truck and light out across the Great Basin searching for the ghost of Desert Jim and that big Palomino, its coat the color of desert sand.

Afterword

I fell in love with the West over the course of several years in the mid 1980s. Through a mix of stubbornness, naiveté, and plain dumb luck, I managed to settle in Wyoming in 1992. Once here, I took the usual road trips to see the civilized sites and hiked the usual mountain trails to see the back county. I realized something was missing in my exploration of my adopted home. None of those trips included time to stop in at the bars that looked so fascinating from the outside, as they sprawled in solitude in a high desert, or the foot of a mountain, or at the mouth of a canyon twenty miles from the nearest town. Those places, I told myself, are where I can learn about the real Wyoming, beyond what I read in the newspapers or glean from Chamber of Commerce sales pitches.

So I dedicated three years of my life to visiting and writing about Wyoming bars. My husband Ronald Hansen is also a settler here, and together we drove around Wyoming seeking out the only bar in town, complete with pickup trucks in the parking lot and a drive-up window for package liquor sales. We parked in the inviting glow of neon beer signs, clomped across board sidewalks, pushed open burglar-barred entrances sawed into Western façades, and sashayed into bars full of strangers who were unapologetically drinking during the day. We found stools at the bar, ordered a Miller Genuine Draft or, if we were at the bar before noon a Coors Light, and announced to the company that we were on a bar tour of Wyoming.

We've been to a lot of the small bars in Wyoming, but the list is inexhaustible. Mountain hamlets nestled among towering lodge pole pine. Havens from blowing high desert dust. Spots born and sustained by mining enterprises. Ranching towns. Places as old as Wyoming's emigrant history. Places deeply connected to Wyoming's indigenous past and Native Americans. Places that are almost in other states.

Everyone has an idea for another place we should visit. We've taken their advice and sometimes found a dandy we never knew was there; other times we bumped along gravel roads miles from any highway only to find that the bar is no longer there, victim of fire or failure.

After I had a pretty good start on this book, I sent a copy of the essay I'd written to the folks at each bar. I asked for any correction of factual error, but more so, any comments they'd like to make. I'm greatly indebted to all those who took the time to reply with corrections or concerns.

Even in the three years we've been traveling this circuit, several bars have changed hands and changed names. I regret not being able to revisit Rowdy's Spirits and Bait, now under new ownership as the Hyattville Bar. The regular customers are still there, as the new owners inform me, but the place has changed quite a bit, and the girlie posters are a thing of the past.

The Tavern in Fort Laramie is in new hands, too. Danny Garhart writes that he sold the place to his good friend Alberta Busking. She's reopened the Bed & Breakfast part of the building and calls the place the Country Cottage Inn. Danny's daughter Lacy and her husband Scott have also sold their bar in Hartville to Mike and Heather Schoning, who also have Mike's Place in Glendo. They plan to restore the bar and make it a thriving business.

And the Cactus Tree Pub's owners, Ed and Jessica, took a look out the window of the bar one day and decided to rename the place Antelope Crossing Pub. Finally, we're saddened to learn of the death of Mike Vinich's daughter Michelle Vinich-Lajeunesse, after a long battle with cancer. We met her very kind husband J.R. during one of our trips to Hudson and we know she'll be missed.

Another change it was not possible to keep up with is the number of drilling rigs, new roads, and sundry pieces of heavy equipment brought to Wyoming by the current energy boom. No sooner are a record number of new gas wells poked into Wyoming's tough outer cover, than another hundred come in and break that record. In addition, coal is dug out from the surface and carted away in trains: chunks of Wyoming's corpus headed east in coal cars bound for eastern plants to be burned to create electricity. Meanwhile, coal bed methane is released from the ground with the sighing sound of air from a balloon.

Our state legislature wonders what to do with all the energy-boom revenue, high school kids bone up for college funded by newly created scholarships, and the pristine waters and clean air of Wyoming will soon be remembered only by the old-timers. But the doors of little mom and pop bar businesses stay open for now, thanks to these new customers.

We've found it is impossible to find and write about and photograph every little bar in Wyoming. Some are open only on weekends, or only during hunting season, or only in the summer. Bars come and go, open and close, unpredictably and without loud public notice. To every bar we should have included in this book but didn't, we beg forgiveness. Although the bar tour book is finished, the bar tour itself never ends.

To all the bartenders and bar customers: If you recognize yourself in these pages, I hope you remember fondly the hours a couple of crazy bar tourists from

Laramie popped in. I hope I have fairly represented everyone's stories that I've included here as part of my own. I hope I told all of our stories in a way that will help readers feel like they, too, have spent some time with the jukeboxes and jackalopes on a Wyoming bar journey.

Printed in the United States
87911LV00002B/181-234/A

9 781932 636345